It has been my pleasure to watch the hand of the Lord on Tom and Marilyn's life. They have been in good standing with the Voice of Revival for the past twenty years. I was privileged to be their first pastor. I would encourage any pastor to extend the right hand of fellowship to them so that you and your congregation might witness the great things the Lord has done.

—KENNETH McCABE, PRESIDENT/GENERAL OVERSEER
KEN McCABE VOICE OF REVIVAL
HASTINGS, MICHIGAN

Although Tom and Marilyn had to experience such terrible tragedy, I am proud of them for allowing God to use them to help others deal with major hurts in their lives. You need to listen to what this couple has to say.

—PASTOR GARY FOLDS
SECOND BAPTIST CHURCH
MACON, GEORGIA

After having heard the testimony of Tom and Marilyn Rose, I must say, their ministry is tremendous. They have a powerful message of hope born out of their commitment to God and a deep compassion for people who are brokenhearted. Theirs is a ministry of encouragement to anyone who has experienced tragedy and a testimony of God's grace to all.

—PASTOR MITCHELL E. CORDER
FLORIDA DIRECTOR OF EVANGELISM AND HOME MISSIONS
CHURCH OF GOD

Tom and Marilyn Rose have ministered in our church with phenomenal results. Our alters were full to overflowing with people saved, filled with the Holy Spirit and healed. Many were blessed by their sensitive heart-felt ministry. They would be a blessing to any church, and I recommend them heartily. God is truly turning tragedy into triumph in their lives.

—PASTOR MIKE THOMAS
PRAISE CATHEDRAL CHURCH OF GOD
PINELLAS PARK, FLORIDA

God has raised this couple's ministry out of the ashes of tragedy — a tragedy the likes I've never personally experienced. They have a message and ministry that encourages even the most discouraged person in the church or community. I recommend Tom's and Marilyn's book to you not only because of their testimony, but also because they have a victorious message for hurting people.

—PASTOR MICHAEL A. MODICA
FIRST ASSEMBLY OF GOD
DeLAND, FLORIDA

Should you have an opportunity to have Tom and Marilyn speak and minister at your church or organization, I wholeheartedly challenge you not to miss that chance. You and your members will receive a blessing you won't soon forget. The Rose family stands as a living testament to the saving, healing power of the love of Jesus Christ.

—BILLY BRUCE
NEWS EDITOR
Charisma and Ministries Today MAGAZINES

As their pastor I have a deep respect for the Roses' relationship with Christ and for their ministry. The Sanctuary Church heartily embraces them as Godly servants. If their ministry could be presented in your church you would be greatly blessed. Brother Tom and Sister Marilyn are used of God to reach many with their message of love, acceptance and forgiveness.

—PASTOR J.D. SIMMONS
DeLAND SANCTUARY CHURCH OF GOD
DeLAND, FLORIDA

Tom and Marilyn Rose's testimony of how God's miracle-working power has sustained, healed and brought them through one crisis after another, proves again and again that God is faithful. Isaiah 59:19 adequately describes their situation: "When the enemy shall come in like a flood, the Spirit of the Lord shall lift up a standard against him."

I heartily recommend Tom and Marilyn's book and their ministry to you!

—DR. HOWARD J. RIDINGS
DIRECTOR OF MINISTRY DEVELOPMENT
STRANG COMMUNICATIONS COMPANY

The Valley of
Decision

Thomas and Marilyn Rose

CREATION
HOUSE
PRESS

THE VALLEY OF DECISION by Thomas and Marilyn Rose
Published by Creation House Press
A part of Strang Communications Company
600 Rinehart Road • Lake Mary, FL 32746
www.creationhouse.com

Unless otherwise indicated, all Scripture quotations are taken from the King James Version.

Scripture quotations marked NIV® are taken from the Holy Bible, New International Version.® Copyright © 1973, 1978, 1984 by International Bible Society. Used by permission of International Bible Society.

"NIV" and "New International Version" are trademarks registered in the United States Patent and Trademark Office by International Bible Society.

Library of Congress Card Number: 00-109360
International Standard Book Number: 0-88419-759-X

0 1 2 3 4 5 6 VERSA 8 7 6 5 4 3 2 1
Printed in the United States of America

DEDICATION

This book is dedicated to Benny and Lacey, our son and daughter, who since 1994 have been enjoying the splendors of heaven. Marilyn and I look forward with great anticipation for the day when we will be reunited for all of eternity with them and with Jesus, our Lord and Savior who made a way for us where there was no other way.

Acknowledgments

Marilyn and I would like to begin by thanking both of our families for all the support they were to us when we needed them the most.

We would also like to express our utmost gratitude to the following church congregations that helped us when we could not help ourselves:

• Beginning with our former pastor, Michael Coleman, and our home church, the DeLand Sanctuary Church of God, that supported us with countless hours of prayer and with newfound friendships when we desperately needed them. For the generous financial support they extended to me and my family, as well as their continued support to our ministry.

• The people of the First Baptist Church of DeLeon Springs for all the food they collected and brought to our family. For the members of their congregations, most of which we had never met, yet they volunteered their time to pack and move our entire household and give what comfort they could.

• St. Barnabas Episcopal Church, whose support has been so consistent over the years. They not only helped us during the time of tragedy, but they also helped us take our story to Africa and Europe. We also thank them for their financial contribution towards this book.

• First Assembly of God of DeLand, Florida, for their friendship over the years, and for their prayers and financial support to our ministry.

• Also to our countless friends who have laughed and cried with us, who have helped us carry the vision and who have supported us while our Lord turned tragedy into triumph.

• Last of all, a special thank you to Ken and Dorothy McCabe, founders of the Voice of Revival and our first pastors who spent endless midnight hours getting us grounded in the Word of God. For the years of spiritual guidance and a constant voice of wisdom in both good and bad times.

Contents

Foreword

GOD'S WORD SAYS HE NEVER GIVES US MORE than we can handle. He challenges us to have faith in Him no matter what happens. He tells us His grace is sufficient for us in any circumstance. He says He causes everything to work together for good for those who love Him.

But when we face tragedy and trauma, we may wonder if God's Word really is true. Is there peace? Is there healing? Dare we ask, is there joy after experiencing horrible, heartbreaking events?

Tom and Marilyn Rose and their daughter, Rachel, are living testaments to the truth of God's Word and to the surety of His faithfulness to all who call upon His Most Holy and worthy name.

The Roses attended the church in DeLand, Florida, where I was a member. I was working as a reporter at the *Daytona Beach News-Journal* on the night of the tragedy that claimed the lives of two of their young children. I was soon writing stories about the

Rose family's plight and how their community rallied around them.

Tom looked bad. He was dying. He needed a new heart. He was on the transplant list at Shands Hospital in Gainesville. To be honest, I didn't think Tom would make it. How could he survive such excruciating grief while at the same time try to live with only 15 percent heart capacity?

Have you ever witnessed a miracle? I mean, a Bible-times, Jesus-sized miracle right before your eyes? It will change your life as it changed mine when I watched God restore Tom and turn his family's tears of grief into uncanny joy. How can these people who suffered so much—losing their business, their home and two of their precious children—be so happy and so willing to serve a God who allowed them to suffer? Because Jesus is who He said He is! And He has given Tom and Marilyn Rose a mission—to show others who've reached the depths of the deepest valley that God is there for them. I saw the Rose family healed, restored and set free, and it changed my life. I pray that this amazing testimony will do the same for you.

—BILLY BRUCE
NEWS EDITOR, *Charisma* MAGAZINE

"Multitudes, multitudes in the valley of decision: for the day of the Lord is near in the valley of decision. The sun and the moon shall be darkened, and the stars shall withdraw their shining. The Lord also shall roar out of Zion, and utter his voice from Jerusalem; and the heavens and the earth shall shake: but the Lord will be the hope of his people, and the strength of the children of Israel."

—JOEL 3:14-16

The Valley of Decision

OEL 3:14–16 IS THE SCRIPTURE ON WHICH I WOULD like to base the personal testimony of my family, for I truly believe there are multitudes and multitudes in the valley of decision. When trouble strikes a family, they feel as if there is no light, and that the sun and the moon and the stars no longer shine for them. This is when they need to see that it is the Lord who will roar out of Zion on their behalf. He will be their hope, but there are decisions to be made, and these decisions will profoundly affect the outcome of whether they survive or throw up their hands and quit—physically, emotionally or spiritually checking out on life.

In 1971, after serving six years in the military and having experienced Vietnam, I had returned to my hometown of Nashville, Michigan. Feeling as if I didn't fit in anymore and looking for a change, I decided to join my brother, Danny, who had started a business in Manitou Springs, Colorado.

It was in Manitou Springs in the summer of 1973 that I met my wife, Marilyn. She had grown up in this picturesque town, which was nestled at the foot of Pike's Peak— in my opinion, one of the most beautiful places I had ever seen. Upon arriving in Manitou, I took a job to supplement my income from my brother's business, and, as chance would have it, I was Marilyn's boss. I remember the first time I saw her come bouncing into the room, her big smile and flashing eyes. Truly, my heart skipped a beat. Of course, I had to play it cool, so it was not until the first day of October that I asked her out.

We dated for some time, and in the following spring I asked Marilyn to marry me. Then, one year later on April 18, 1975, Marilyn and I were married. By this time, we had decided to open a retail outlet of our own. We did well financially, but our lives were in turmoil. Our store was in a prime tourist location, and there was money to be made from early morning to late at night. To keep up the pace, we began relying on drugs. It did not take long until the drugs had taken over our lives. At this time we decided to try to escape the crowd with which we were running. We returned to Michigan to see if we could get our lives back on course.

It was during this time, on March 15, 1977, that Jesus came into our lives. Marilyn and I gave our hearts to the Lord on the same day. Having experienced what the world had to offer, we had no desire to return, so we plunged headlong into getting to know and serve our Lord. During my teen years, and for a short time after my military service, I had played drums professionally. I took this talent and used it for the Lord. Because of my musical ability, an evangelist from Bradenton, Florida, asked us to join his team. We worked with him for some time before finally settling in St. Petersburg where we served as musicians, church bus drivers, youth leaders, Sunday school teachers and anything else we could find to do.

On December 15, 1981, an event happened that changed our lives. Our first daughter, Lacey Jane, was born. It was no longer just Marilyn and me being footloose and fancy-free. We were now a family, and I loved it! Our family continued to grow with the birth of our son, Benjamin, three years later on December 8, 1984. To round it all out, on June 21, 1986, Rachel was born. We felt that our quiver was full, and we were truly blessed. I can remember those Wednesday night church services, going from classroom to classroom picking up the children. I was so proud; I felt as if I were ten feet tall.

By the time Rachel was born, we had moved from St. Petersburg to the Orlando, Florida, area where we started a sign business. Again, the Lord blessed us. Our business prospered. It was not a large sign shop, but we had the freedom to have our children with us, and we earned enough to spend several weeks a year either at Disney or at the beach enjoying our family.

I can remember Marilyn during this time in our lives praying, "Don't come yet, Jesus. Let us get our children raised. I want to see our girls get married and see Benjamin graduate from the Air Force Academy. Don't come yet."

"These things I have spoken unto you, that in me ye might have peace. In the world ye shall have tribulation: but be of good cheer; I have overcome the world."

—JOHN 16:33

2

Troubled Times

IN THE SPRING OF 1994, THE TIDE BEGAN TO TURN. Our sign business required me to spend much of my time working outside in the Florida heat. I would route or sand-blast signs in temperatures sometimes exceeding 90 degrees with high humidity, so I didn't think too much of it when it seemed as if my body were slowing down on me. I was now forty-eight years old, and I thought maybe I just couldn't "cut the mustard" anymore.

Then, ever so slowly, I began to experience flu-like symptoms, but not enough to warrant staying in bed. For the first time in our business career, I failed to get orders finished on time. Of course, being self-employed, our income suffered. By the end of July, my condition deteriorated to the point that I could hardly work. Marilyn began pressuring me to see a doctor.

I have nothing against doctors, but, my symptoms were nothing drastic—fatigue, slight nausea and slight chest congestion.

My excuse was, "I have a flu bug, and it'll go away. I just need to rest."

By this time, our income was almost non-existent. Marilyn was to the point of selling all the antiques, jewelry and anything else of value we collected over the years so that we could pay for our living expenses. The business overhead continued as well.

After I spent almost two weeks on bed rest, Marilyn went to work at the sign shop with our two girls. She had left our son, Ben, with me because I promised her that if I was not feeling better by that night I would see a doctor. About the time I expected her to return home, I managed to get out of bed and dress myself. However, the truth was that I had found it increasingly difficult to breathe throughout the day. It was to the point that my son had to prop me up with pillows so that if I dozed off I could get my breath. However, being as hard-headed as I was, I met her at the door and proceeded to tell her I felt much better. She looked at me for a minute and turned to Benjamin.

"Is this true, Benny? Has he been better today?"

Well, I was busted. Ben proceeded to tell her about having to prop me up with pillows so I could breathe, upon which she told me to get in the car. I began with my usual excuses. This time they held no weight.

"You promised me," she retorted. "Either you would truly be better or you would go to the doctor. Now I expect you to keep your word."

That day I knew something was horribly wrong. I could hear that rattle in my chest. In Vietnam, I had flown many medical missions, and I was familiar with what we called the "death rattle," but I just didn't want to believe I could be that sick. I didn't want to face what a doctor might tell me. I just kept hanging on to the thought that it would go away.

At first I thought I had won a reprieve from the dreaded doctor's appointment. It was after five on a Saturday, and surely there wasn't any way Marilyn could find a doctor at this late hour, but she did. She called several emergency care centers and found one just beginning to close. She persuaded them to stay open a few minutes longer until we could get to the center.

When I arrived at the office, they began to do the routine checks. The nurse weighed me in. I was surprised with how much I weighed. I had not eaten that much lately, but my weight seemed to be high. Then she took my blood pressure. She pumped it up. Listened carefully, she gave me a puzzled look and did it again. After taking the second reading she jotted it down, not saying a word.

Then she said, "I think I should measure your oxygen intake."

I had never experienced this before. She retrieved a small device and slipped it on my finger. After several moments she took it off and shook it. Then she proceeded to try it again. She took it off and put it on her own finger.

Her remark was, "Well, it's working."

At this, she left the room to call the doctor. Almost immediately the doctor returned, holding the chart.

He listened to my chest, asked me a few questions, and turned to my wife, "I want you to get him to the hospital right now. At best he has a severe case of pneumonia, but I am more inclined to believe that he is experiencing heart failure."

At this I began with my objections, "Heart failure, the hospital, I don't think so. Maybe tomorrow—if I don't feel better, I'll go tomorrow."

The doctor looked me straight in the eye and said,

"If you don't go now you will never see tomorrow."

He again turned to my wife, "I am going to write you a note. As soon as you get to the hospital, give it to them."

Upon paying our bill, the doctor handed Marilyn a sealed envelope, and we were out the door. Now, everyone who knows me realizes just how hard-headed I can be, so I thought I would give it one last shot. Upon getting into the car I told Marilyn to take me home so I could shower and at least clean up.

Her reply was, "I am not your mother! You do not need to take a bath and put on clean underwear to go to the hospital. We are going, and we are going now!"

On the short trip to the hospital I found myself growing weaker and weaker. I told Marilyn to drop me off at the front door and I would wait for her while she parked the car. I can remember hanging onto the rail going into the lobby. I felt as if I would collapse any second. Marilyn rushed up and helped me in. She handed the lady at the front desk the note from the doctor. She opened it and quickly went to the back room, returning with a male nurse who ushered me back.

After they made me lie down, everything began to blur. I remember the nurse talking with a doctor on the phone. He had hooked me up to a machine, which continually read my blood pressure. I could not see what it said, because it was behind me.

I could hear the nurse saying, "Yes, I am sure that is what it says. I took a reading by hand, and I am looking at the machine now. Yes, he is conscious."

That was the last thing I remember before falling unconscious. The next thing I remember is waking up in the morning hooked up to all kinds of gadgets.

Nurses were coming in probing, and Marilyn was sitting there watching over me. I discovered I had congestive heart failure and came very close to death's door. They were still running tests trying to discover just what had been the cause, but although I was still in critical condition in the intensive care unit, I was stable.

After a battery of tests the doctors concluded that my body was a mess. They said my kidneys had shut down, which was the reason for my weight being high. Through the use of diuretics, they took thirty pounds of water off me in about ten days. My liver was inflamed and swollen, which accounted for the yellowish color of my skin.

My lungs had filled with fluid, and my heart had enlarged. Last of all, my thyroid was barely functioning. Besides that, I was doing OK. No, all kidding aside, I finally realized just how sick I was. Yet, the prognosis was not too bad. My doctor felt that my slow thyroid had caused all of my troubles. Although it would take some time, he felt that through the use of medications I would make a complete recovery.

So, after a ten-day stay in the hospital, they released me to the care of my wife, sending me home with a list of medications and orders to stay in bed.

Although I was somewhat out of danger, things at home were getting harder and harder to manage. For years Marilyn had operated a small sideline business of ceramics. She is an excellent painter, and in an attempt to boost our income, she decided to try to increase this endeavor. Although sales were good, it was very labor intensive.

Between taking care of me and the children, and

managing the sinking sign business, she found herself over her head in work. Struggling to keep everything in a balance, you might say the scale was tipped when it was "Mother to the rescue!" You know how moms can be when a firstborn son is sick. My mom is no different. So, down she came from Michigan. Luckily, Marilyn and my mom get along quite well. She was also able to help with things around the house, while her husband, Joe, helped Marilyn with the sign shop and ceramic business.

Two weeks after my release from the hospital I awoke to many of the same symptoms I had experienced earlier. The day before I went to the doctor's office everything seemed to be fine, but today was different from the others. I felt extremely tired, and I was having some difficulty breathing. Marilyn told me I looked awfully pale. We were somewhat guarded, but we weren't overly concerned until that evening when we went to bed. Marilyn laid her head on my chest and could hear that familiar rattle.

She insisted we make a trip to the emergency room, where they confirmed I was having another heart failure. They kept me in the hospital another week and readjusted my medications. They continued to affirm that it was due to the thyroid and that with time I would make a full recovery. But the following week I was stricken with a third heart failure, this one being the worst of them all. By this time, my doctors were baffled as to what was going on with me. My liver seemed to be recovering. The thyroid medication had my hormone count leveled, yet my heart continued to deteriorate. Each time I experienced a heart failure, the muscle enlarged and the percentage it was able to contract went lower.

The doctors decided that it was time for me to see a group of heart specialists in the Orlando area, so they transferred me to Florida Hospital in Orlando. I underwent a full battery of tests there, from a heart biopsy to bone marrow biopsies, full-body CAT-scans, and every kind of blood test imaginable. They kept me there a little over a week. Although all of the prodding and probing was uncomfortable, I was determined to make the best of it. I joked with the doctors and nurses, making light of their endless efforts to find out what was going on with me. After days of testing, the heart specialist entered my room. He shut the door and pulled up a chair. His words rang loud and clear in my spirit.

"Mr. Rose, I am sorry to tell you, but there is no hope for you outside of a heart transplant. Some sort of virus has attacked your body. We have not been able to determine what the virus is. It might have been something you contracted recently, or it quite possibly could have been a virus you picked up overseas in Vietnam. Sometimes a virus can stay dormant in your system for years. Then, all of a sudden, it will come alive and ravage a body. Although the virus seems to be gone, it has damaged the heart muscle itself. At the present time, your heart is only contracting at 15% of normal capacity. There isn't a thing we can do for you except attempt to give you a new heart. They are calling your wife to pick you up. We will be releasing you today. I will be sending all your medical reports to the transplant department at Shands Hospital at the University of Florida in Gainesville. This will take approximately ten days, after which they will contact you for an appointment for a heart evaluation to see if you are eligible to be put on the transplant list."

I felt as if a bomb had exploded in my head. I kept hearing the words "no hope." I struggled desperately to get my thoughts together to face Marilyn and the kids. I kept wondering where was the Lord in all of this. For years Marilyn and I had worked in the church, we had seen the Lord answer countless prayers and had seen people healed. Why was this all happening to me? I had a wife and children to think about. *Why me?*

All during my three hospital stays I witnessed about my faith in Jesus, and how I believed everything was going to be OK. Now all I had was this sinking feeling. What made matters worse was that news of my prognosis had spread to the nursing staff. Although they were quite professional, we had made friends over the past several days. Now as they entered my room, I could see where they had been crying.

The hospital did not tell Marilyn over the phone the reason for my release, so the news came as a complete shock. She normally spent the mornings and late evenings at the hospital. The remainder of the day she spent trying to keep the household together. So when they asked her to come in that afternoon because I was being released, she thought it was good news. It did not take her long to figure out something was up. As she walked through the intensive care unit, she was not met with the usual cheery greetings with which she had grown accustomed. I remember her entering my room with a puzzled look on her face.

"What's up? I got a call that they're going to send you home today."

I did my best to keep a stiff upper lip as I explained what the doctor had told me, but it was to no avail. When she began to cry, I could no longer hold back the floodgate of tears. Shortly after this, the doctor reappeared with the list of instructions for her to follow, the gist of them being to keep me in bed and *stress free* until we heard from Shands.

The trip from Orlando to our home in DeLand takes about forty-five minutes. Marilyn cried all the way. It seemed to be more then she could handle. All of the stress of the household, the business and now this news was more than she could take. It all seemed to come crashing down.

She kept saying, "I thought everything was going to be all right. I'm really not prepared for this. What are we going to do?"

Unfortunately, I didn't have any answers. I knew my chances for receiving a new heart were slim. I knew my own heart was deteriorating fast. There was no question about that. Would I be eligible? How could we pay for such an operation? We had no insurance and no money. What were we to do now?

By the time the kids arrived home from school, Marilyn had managed to pull herself together. She was determined to keep things in the house as light and near normal as possible. She tried to explain what I was doing home, and how I would need an operation. For the time being, we would all have to do our best not to agitate one another. This was asking a lot. We had our three children, ages 8, 9 and 12 in the house.

My mother and her husband where there most of the time. They had purchased a mobile home to stay in not far from our house, and then one of my sisters had come in from Colorado to try to help us. Needless to say, Marilyn had her hands full.

Marilyn has always been at her best when she has something to do. When she takes on a project, she is like a little bulldog. She will work endlessly to accomplish whatever the task is at hand. She decided to meet the challenge head on. She went to work to find any financial help we might be entitled to in order for me to get the medical assistance I needed. She had stacks of paperwork from Social Security, but what she was most thankful for was the response she was getting from the Veterans Administration. Having been a paratrooper assigned to the First Air Calvary, I had flown a lot of combat hours and received numerous commendations.

When Marilyn took my DD/214 form into their office, the clerk's response was, "This is obviously a man who was in the heat of the battle in Vietnam. He risked his life for us. We are going to do as much as we can for him, now that his life is on the line."

The woman who helped Marilyn was a Christian, and I know that the Lord gave us favor with her. It was September 29, 1994, when Marilyn received an appointment to file my case.

She was told, "We need to get this claim filed by tomorrow night. If we can do that, you will receive benefits for the whole month of September. The office closes at 5:00. I should be finished with my last appointment today around 4:30. If you return at that time, I will stay late and help you with the paperwork. In the meantime, here is a list of things we will need. Contact his doctors and tell them you need all his records and that you will be coming in to get them."

Marilyn did as she was told, although some of the medical records would not be available until the next day. The two of them worked until about 6:30 that evening. She told her to come again the next day and they would finish.

"I will call the administration office and tell them we will be faxing this report in to them and ask them not to leave until they receive it."

They managed somehow to get everything filed and faxed in time. This was September 30, ten days since they had released me from the hospital. Marilyn came home that night lighthearted. She felt confident we would get some kind of help from the V.A., and the generous help she had received from them encouraged her.

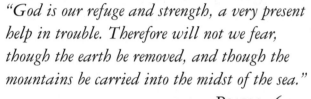

"God is our refuge and strength, a very present help in trouble. Therefore will not we fear, though the earth be removed, and though the mountains be carried into the midst of the sea."

—PSALM 46:1–2

3

God Is Our Refuge

Upon Marilyn's arrival home from the V.A., the house was buzzing with activity. Marilyn, in her effort to keep some sort of a routine in the kids' life, had told them they could go to the skating rink that evening. Friday night had always been roller skating night at our house. Even Marilyn and I would participate sometimes.

Lacey had two friends over who were going with her to the skating rink. Ben had his skates on and was "warming up," as he called it. My sister Vickie was there, and Rachel, our youngest, was in bed with me. (Rachel would hardly leave my side. As soon as she would get home from school, she would plop her backpack on the floor beside my bed and climb in to watch afternoon cartoons with me. Once, she even stowed away in Marilyn's car so she could visit me in the hospital. It was during my second hospital stay, and Rachel pretended to have a stomachache and asked to stay home from school. My mother was with us at the time and volunteered to watch Rachel while Marilyn went to be with me at the hospital. Marilyn drove away in her car, not realizing that Rachel had sneaked out of the house and had hidden in the back seat. After Marilyn got all the way to the hospital, Rachel appeared, barefoot and in her pajamas. Marilyn was not sure what to do with her. Children really were not allowed in intensive care, and besides that she was not even dressed. Thank God, Marilyn was bringing me a pair of slippers that day, so she put them on Rachel, marched her up to the nurses' station and pleaded her case. They all got a big chuckle out of it and allowed her in to see me.)

As I was saying, the house was all a buzz. Ben and Lacey now joined their sister in my bedroom to see me before they left for the skating rink. Ben, who had wavy hair just like mine, was after me to help him comb it. He was under the impression that no one could comb his hair like his papa could. And, of course, he had to be "looking good" for the skating rink. Besides that, for a young man of nine, he could grow the longest sideburns, and they really needed trimming. Against objections from Marilyn, I agreed to get up and comb his hair and trim his sideburns. With a heart at fifteen percent, this was quite a task, but it was my pleasure to be able to do it. Upon finishing Ben's hair, I returned to bed, when the phone rang.

It was Karen, one of my sisters, calling from Michigan. Lacey answered the phone. She proceeded to tell her aunt that she and Ben, along with two other girlfriends, were going to the skating rink.

Karen must have asked Lacey about her little brother tagging along with them. Lacey replied, "Oh no! I don't mind taking Benny. He's cool. I take Benny everywhere." And she did.

She would take Ben anywhere she went without complaining. Marilyn and I put an end to Benjamin attending slumber parties with his sister. When he was little it was cute, but now he was almost ten years old, and spending the night with a bunch of girls wasn't right.

After a short phone conversation with Karen, Marilyn stuck her head in the door and told the kids she would drive them to the skating rink. It was at this time that my sister, Vickie, shouted from the other room, "Marilyn you just stay home and enjoy your dinner with Tom. You've been out all day getting everything filed. Just relax, and I will take the kids for you."

Marilyn quickly agreed, "But please take my car. Your van does not have seat belts for all the kids." Marilyn always insisted the kids buckle up. Vickie had a cargo van that was not equipped to carry that many children at one time.

Ben and Lacey told me they loved me, gave their mom a big hug, and went out the door with their friends. Within minutes, Marilyn came in the room with our dinner. She sat down and we began to go over the events of the day. She told me how hopeful she was that things were going to turn around for us. It was during our meal that we began to hear a number of emergency vehicles pass our house. We lived only a block away from a state highway so we often heard the scream of sirens as they passed.

We finished our meal, when Marilyn began to get a little nervous that Vickie had not returned. But Vickie was known to try to accomplish several errands while she was out, so we were not too concerned and continued our chat. Then we heard the sound of a helicopter. It sounded as if it were landing somewhere close by. It was about this time that the phone rang. It was my mother on the other end.

"Marilyn, I am so glad you are home. Joe and I were returning from the store when we came upon a terrible accident up on the main intersection from the house. They were diverting all the traffic, but I thought I saw your car. I knew you were planning on taking the kids to the skating rink, and I was so frightened it might have been you and the kids in the accident."

Marilyn's face turned pale. "I didn't take the kids. Vickie drove them in my car. I'm sorry, Mom, but I have to go now."

Somehow Marilyn composed herself and said, "Tom, that was your mother. There seems to be some sort of accident on the corner. I'm going out there and see what is going on. I'll be right back."

At this point this story must be told in Marilyn's own words. We did not discuss the events of this night because of my condition. I remained at home with Rachel through the next few hours.

"*Peace I leave with you, my peace I give unto you: not as the world giveth, give I unto you. Let not your heart be troubled, neither let it be afraid.*"

—JOHN 14:27

4

He Is Our Peace

As I (Marilyn) left the house, my head was spinning. I was not sure what to do. I wanted to get down to that intersection as quickly as possible. It was about half a mile away, so I went to one of our neighbors and asked them to give me a ride up to the corner. She quickly agreed. We jumped into her car and pulled out of the subdivision where we live. Almost as soon as we got on the main road we were caught in the traffic, which the police were trying to turn around. I could not stand it so I jumped out of the car and began running to the intersection. I can remember running as hard as I could. I knew there were all kinds of traffic around me, but all I could hear was the beating of my heart and the jolt of my feet as they pounded the ground. As I approached the intersection, I saw that emergency vehicles had encircled the cars like a wagon train under attack. A policeman came out of nowhere and grabbed me by the arm.

"What do you think you are doing, lady?" he shouted.

I remember whirling around and bursting out in tears, as I recognized my wrecked car in the middle of the accident scene.

"That's my car, and those are my children in there!"

The policeman's first response was a muffled, "Oh, my God."

He then took me by both arms and got real close to my face, "You can't go over there. They won't even let us go over right now. They are doing everything they can to get your children out of the car."

He looked up now and said, "How did you get here? Are you with someone in this line of traffic?"

I said yes and described my neighbor's car. He told me he would send a man to get her out of the traffic and we could pull up in the median.

"You just sit here in the car. I will be sure to inform you of everything I can."

In my heart, I desperately wanted to run over to the car, but I knew I would only hinder their efforts to rescue my children. The policeman informed me right away that they had already airlifted the driver (Vickie) to Orlando, and that they had also airlifted two of the girls to a major hospital on the Coast. My daughter was one of them. The third girl was not as severely injured, so she was taken by ambulance to a local hospital in DeLand. At the time, I didn't think to ask the policeman how he knew that the child who wasn't as severely injured was not my daughter. I later discovered that the girl's father was a paramedic there on the scene. The emergency's team main concern was now Benjamin.

"The little boy is pinned in the car. They are having to cut him out."

It took over an hour for them to free him from the

car. It felt like an eternity to me.

Once they got him free, the officer returned and said, "They will be airlifting your son to the Coast. Two of the girls are already there, so you should leave right now."

The police managed to get us turned around and out of the traffic. My neighbor, Brenda, told me she would take me to the hospital. I told her I had better stop and see Tom for a minute. I was not sure what I would say. I knew I had to tell him I was headed for the hospital, but I did not want to alarm him because of his weak condition. When we pulled into the driveway, Rachel was waiting for me in the yard. She was frightened and crying uncontrollably. She kept calling for Lacey.

"Momma, take me with you. I want to see Lacey. Take me with you, Momma, please take me," she begged.

I stooped down and told her that there wasn't anyone else to be with Papa right now and that she had to stay and be a big girl and watch over her Papa. I knew if she were there, Tom would try to stay calm for her sake, and I really did not know what I would be facing once I got to the hospital.

The hospital is approximately twenty-four miles from DeLand, but I know we did it in record time. When we arrived in the emergency room, there seemed to be a lot of commotion going on. The parents of the other child had already received the news and were there. The mother was somewhat hysterical. She kept screaming that she wanted to see her daughter. I immediately went to the desk to inform the nurse who I was. She asked me again if I was Mrs. Rose, the mother who had just left the scene of the accident. I told her I was, and she asked me to wait for just a minute. Within seconds, a doctor appeared.

"Mrs. Rose, we have been receiving calls from the hospital in DeLand. It seems that they were having trouble getting your son stabilized. As soon as they can, they will be airlifting him to the Arnold Palmer Hospital for Children in Orlando. They want you to come as soon as possible to DeLand. They say he is quite critical."

I felt as if my knees were going to buckle. Then my thoughts turned to Lacey.

"What about my daughter? How is she?" I asked.

"I really can't tell you anything right now. We have two young girls back there in critical condition. They are both the same age, and we are not sure which one is which."

Again in the background, I could hear the cries of the other mother.

"Can't you let someone go back and identify the girls? I am here right now, and I would like a little information before I have to go to DeLand."

The doctor looked around, not knowing what to say. I then turned and saw the father of Lacey's friend. He was calm. He looked to be somewhat in shock, but he was sitting calmly.

"How about if you let him go in. He can tell you which girl is which."

The doctor agreed. Within minutes, they returned.

The doctor said, "I am not going to lie: your daughter is in critical condition, but from the calls we have been receiving from DeLand, I feel like you had better go there. Here is my number." He handed me a card. "Once things have calmed down just a little you can call me. I don't care what time of night it might be. Just call and I will give you as much information on your daughter as I can."

Brenda and I headed back to her car. We raced silently back to DeLand, neither of us knowing what to say. Everything kept whirling around my head.

So many doctors, so many words:, "Your son is in very critical condition." "I'm not going to lie, your daughter is in critical condition." "Take your husband home and be sure to keep him stress free."

My head was spinning, and here we were racing from hospital to hospital. When we got to DeLand, Brenda dropped me off at the emergency room door and went to park the car.

When I came in a nurse met me, "Are you Mrs. Rose?"

I told her who I was and that I wanted to see my son.

"I'm sorry, but you can't right now. Would you like to see our minister who is on staff? Can we call your husband for you? Or maybe your pastor?"

"No, I do not want you to call anyone. My husband is at home, in need of a heart transplant. He must not find out what is going on yet. When can I see my son?"

During our conversation, she was leading me back to a doctor's conference room, and finally told me, "Just wait in here, Mrs. Rose. Someone will be in shortly."

I couldn't tell you how long she was gone. When she returned, I was just sitting there, in some state of shock, I suppose.

"The helicopter is on its way to take your son to Orlando," the nurse began.

"Can't I see him now?" I pleaded.

"Mrs. Rose, we still do not have him cleaned up, and besides that, he is unconscious. He will not know you are there."

"I don't care. I really want to see him," I continued to plead.

"OK, you do seem calm, so maybe I could let you go in there for just a minute. They will be coming with the helicopter any minute anyway."

The nurse escorted me into another room. They had Benjamin lying on a gurney. His head was in some sort of brace. He looked so small lying there. I walked up to him and took him by the hand.

"Benny, it's Mommy. I'm here and everything is going to be all right."

At the sound of my voice, tears began to flow out of the corners of his eyes, which were swollen shut. I knew then that he heard me. Immediately after I had spoken just these few words, the airlift team entered the room.

"Mrs. Rose, you are going to have to go. We must move your son."

Just a minute, I whispered, and I turned to Benny again, "Ben, you are going to go on a helicopter now."

Since Tom had ridden in helicopters in Vietnam, this had been one of Benny's dreams: to ride a helicopter.

"They will be taking you to Orlando, and Momma will be right behind them. It's going to be all right, Benny."

Then I quoted a verse he had heard many times, "You know, Benny, that, 'God has not given us the spirit of fear, but of power and of love, Benny, and of a sound mind,' Everything is going to be all right."

Benny's tears continued to roll. With all his might, he slightly lifted one shoulder then the other. I felt that he was trying to protest. They had his head braced, so he had to protest with his shoulders.

At that the paramedics took me by the arm, "I'm sorry, but we really must insist that you leave now. You can see him again in Orlando."

"For I am persuaded, that neither death, nor life, nor angels, nor principalities, nor powers, nor things to come, nor height, nor depth, nor any other creature, shall be able to separate us from the love of God, which is in Christ Jesus our Lord."

—ROMANS 8:38–39

5

God's Grace Is Sufficient

I DON'T KNOW HOW WE DID IT, BUT WE ARRIVED AT the hospital before the helicopter. During the time I was waiting to see Benny, I tried to get my thoughts together enough to make some calls. The first was to my mother in St. Petersburg, Florida. I told her there had been an accident and that Lacey and Ben had been taken to two separate hospitals.

"Mom, I am here with Benjamin. Would you please go to the other hospital to be with Lacey? I want someone there with her. I don't know what I'm going to do about Tom. I'm going to have to call and tell him something, but would you go to Daytona?"

She quickly agreed, and asked, "How bad is it, Marilyn? Do I need to prepare to stay for a while?"

"I think so, Mom. Things don't seem to be looking real good. I don't have a lot of information right now, but plan to stay."

After I spoke with my mother, I made the dreaded call to Tom. I was very evasive. I told him I did not have much information.

"They have been taken to different hospitals. As soon as I know something I will call. Don't worry, Honey; just try to get some rest. Right now everything is under control. Mom is going to the hospital to be with Lacey.

I told him that they had not let me see Ben yet, but that everything would be all right. Just minutes after talking with Tom I received a call from my sister, Carol, who also lived in St. Petersburg. She told me that she and her husband, Steve, were getting ready to leave to come and stay with me.

"You really don't need to be alone right now. We will be there just as soon as we can."

I was thankful for that. I really needed someone. Brenda was still with me, but I could tell she just really did not know what to say or what to do. Thank God she stayed until Steve and Carol arrived.

When I finally was allowed in to see Benny, I realized why it had taken them so long to fly him to Orlando. Although they did not tell me, I believe they had to hook him to life support before they ever moved him. There was no response from him now, and he was hooked to machines to do his breathing, which he previously did not have. They kept him in the emergency room for several hours. During this time, the doctor tried to prepare me for the worst. He told me that Benjamin had suffered severe head trauma, and it would take a miracle for him to survive, but he added that miracles do happen.

I truly believe that Benjamin was brain dead at this time, but the hospital had already received news of my husband's condition and that I had a daughter hospitalized in critical condition. I believe they knew I needed time to sort things out, so they decided to move him to intensive care.

I felt as if I were walking through a nightmare. I was numb. There were no tears, no crying. I just remember feeling extremely cold. The nurses got me a blanket to wrap up in. Dazed, I paced the floors, knowing I had to pull myself together enough to figure out what to do. The night made way to the morning dawn. Tom would soon awake, and I really needed some advice, so I decided to inform his doctors as to what was going on. I put a call through to the answering service. Within minutes I received a reply.

The doctor told me, "You are going to have to break the news to him slowly. He will never be able to handle you telling him he has lost a child without dealing with it a little at a time. Is there anyone there with him who can pick up a prescription?"

"Yes, I think so," I replied.

"I will order a sedative. After you feel you have given enough time for someone to get the prescription to him, and he has had it in his system at least an hour, call him. Tell him things don't look too good. That is all you are to tell him," he said firmly.

"Let him deal with that first. Later, call him and say, 'Things aren't getting any better.' Do this several times. Then, if the worst happens, go home and tell him. He will need you."

After calling home, I had discovered that our neighbor, who was a respiratory therapist, had stayed with him that evening. Also, our pastor had received news of the accident as well as several friends, so the Lord had already provided comfort and support. I told them what the doctors had told me and that they were not to let Tom know I had called. I would call him later.

As the hours rolled on, I sat beside Benny as the

machine rhythmically pumped air in and out of his lungs. I remember looking at him and wishing I had the faith of Elisha, that I could lay my body on him and he would be healed, but I knew I didn't have that kind of faith. It was at this time that I first felt God's "amazing grace," a peace that passed beyond my understanding. The sunlight streaming in the window seemingly cast aside the darkness that had previously filled the room. In my mind, I knew everything I was facing, yet there was such a peace. I even began to sing the song, *Surely the Presence of the Lord Is in This Place.* Even the nurses, as they came to check Ben, mentioned how peaceful it felt in the room.

I did not realize it at the time, but later when I reflected on that day, I realized why Paul, a man who had faith to raise the dead and to shake the viper off of his arm, never wrote, "My *faith* is sufficient," but instead wrote, "God's *grace* is sufficient." (See 2 Corinthians 12:9.) When you discover your situation far out-measures your faith, it is then that God's grace comes in and fills in the gap.

You begin to understand why Paul went on to say, "For I am persuaded, that neither death [not the death of a son or a daughter, a husband or a wife, a mother or a father], nor life, nor angels, nor principalities, nor powers, nor things present [nothing I might be experiencing right now], nor things to come (not those things that worry me or that I might fear), nor height, nor depth, nor any other creature, shall be able to separate us from the love of God, which is in Christ Jesus our Lord" (Rom. 8:38–39).

It was not my faith that brought peace into the room, but rather God's grace. It wasn't until late that afternoon the doctor entered the room.

"Mrs. Rose, I am afraid your son is brain dead. He has been for some time. We heard of your husband's condition, and we were checking with Shands Hospital to see if they could use your son's heart. They told us that if they could, there would never be a better match. They told us that they would forgo all preliminary testing, but when we got down to the details, Ben's heart was just to small for Tom to use. There can only be a 20% weight difference between the donor and the receiver. I know all this is hard for you, but a representative from Trans-life is here if you would like to consider donating Benjamin's organs. I am afraid there isn't anything else we can do for him, and your family needs you."

I agreed to donate Benny's organs. It was one of the hardest things I have ever done; yet I can truly say I am so glad I did. Weeks later when I needed encouragement, a letter came from Trans-life, which told us a thirteen-year-old girl was alive and doing well after receiving Ben's heart. In addition to that, an eighteen-month-old baby girl had received his liver. Finally, a fifty-year-old man and fifty-one-year-old woman were now off of dialysis because of his kidneys. This all may sound gruesome, but we really felt comfort that Benny had been able to help life go on.

After signing the papers, I entered Benjamin's room one last time. The nurses told me that a pastor from one of the local Assemblies of God was there and that he would pray with me if I wanted him to. Upon my agreement, the pastor, Steve, Carol and I entered Benny's room. I remember standing beside his bed. My head bowed as the pastor prayed. Tears flowed out of my eyes as I had never experienced before. They were literally like a river. I couldn't tell you a word that was spoken. I just stood there watching my tears make a puddle on the blanket that covered Benny. I finally heard the word "amen." I lifted my head, bent over and kissed Benny on the cheek, and told him I loved him. With that, I turned and walked out of the room, hearing the whoosh of the respirator as I stepped into the hallway.

Upon exiting the intensive care unit, I was met by Fred and Cindy, a couple from the market where we had our sign business. Fred took one look in my eyes and knew the news wasn't good. I whispered, "Benny's gone." That was all I could get out. Fred threw his arms around me and began to weep. Fred and Cindy had three grown boys of their own and were especially attached to Benny. They were an Italian couple and, as most Italians are, were very passionate. Fred still weeping in my arms, I looked over at Cindy. She had her hand held over her mouth, a look of shock in her eyes.

Suddenly, Fred realized his emotion. "Marilyn, I'm so sorry. I didn't mean to react this way."

I was surprised myself with the numbness that seemed to have enveloped me. I told them both that it was all right but that I really had to go. The thought of telling Tom was weighing heavily on my mind.

On the ride home, it seemed odd that life outside of the hospital was so normal. My whole world had fallen apart, yet I felt as if no one knew. I rode in silence in the back seat, trying to go over in my head what I would tell Tom, but it just would not come. My mind bounced from one scene to another from the previous night. I wondered how Lacey was. How was my mother handling things? What was I to say to Rachel? I didn't have a clue. It would just have to take its course, as everything else had in the past twenty-four hours.

When we pulled into the driveway, Rachel ran out to meet me, her eyes wide with questions as to what was happening. I was at a loss for how to begin.

I stooped down next to the front door. "Rachel, Benny has gone to be with the Lord."

The words just seemed to tumble out. I wanted to say more. I wanted to somehow fill in with some kind of words of comfort, but they just weren't there. Rachel looked stunned. Tears came streaming down her face as she clung to my chest. I don't remember her saying a thing. She just cried.

I held her for a few minutes. Then I said, "We have to go in now. I have to talk to Papa."

I am not sure what happened next. I don't remember who was there or what was said. I just remember entering our bedroom. I had called several times that day, as the doctor had instructed. Tom was now sedated and sound asleep. I sat beside him and touched his shoulder.

"Tom, Tom," I said softly. He awoke and turned a weary face toward me. "Benny's gone; he's gone to be with the Lord."

I could not hold back my tears. Tom let out a cry and wrapped me in his arms, "Oh, Marilyn," he cried.

We just sat there for several minutes, rocking in one another's arms, crying.

Then Tom drew back and spoke. "Marilyn, you know the Lord said that all things work together for good to them that love Him. We have to believe that. Today is the anniversary of our first date. That was nineteen years ago, and it seems like yesterday. Time passes so swiftly. We have to remember the Lord never made us to live in time, to pass through this life so quickly. That was never His plan. He made us to be eternal, and it won't be long until we will all be together again."

We held each other for a while longer and then my thoughts turned toward Lacey. It had been almost twenty-four hours since I had left the hospital where Lacy was. I had spoken with the head surgeon of the trauma team who had given me his card. He told me that Lacey was stable, but he also said the next forty-eight hours would be crucial. Twenty-four of those forty-eight had already passed. I needed to get to her. I persuaded Tom to stay home with Rachel, promising to return as soon as I could. I believe the sedation helped him to agree to stay home.

When I arrived at the hospital, my mother met me. She had spent all night there with Lacey. Lacey, like Benjamin, had also suffered an injury to her head, along with a fractured shoulder, and one of her lungs had collapsed. They had her on a respirator, and they were trying to keep her sedated. I immediately noticed that she was strapped to the bed. I did not understand this until the morphine began to wear off, and she began violently trying to sit up. Her eyes were open, but wild-looking. The nurses rushed in and gave her another shot of morphine.

"We have called for an anesthesiologist. When she gets here, she will put your daughter on a constant drip that will keep her sedated, allowing her body to begin to respond to the medications and begin healing."

I was relieved when they were able to accomplish this. By this time, I was ready to collapse. The nurses told me I really should go home.

"Try to rest Mrs. Rose. We will call you if there is any change in her condition."

With my mother's encouragement and promise to

keep watch, I left for home. By this time, it was around midnight on Saturday night. I climbed into bed beside Tom.

When he awoke, I told him, "Honey, I'm just too tired to talk. I really want to go to early morning service tomorrow. I need to go to church. We'll talk tomorrow."

"Yea, though I walk through the valley of the shadow of death, I will fear no evil; for thou art with me."

—PSALM 23:4

6

Walking Through Shadows

The narrative resumes from Tom's perspective.

ARILYN AWOKE EARLY THE NEXT MORNING and was determined to go to church. She said that she just needed to be in the presence of the Lord. I informed her to come home and pick me up before going to the hospital to see Lacey. The doctors had told her it wasn't a good idea for me to see our daughter in critical condition, but I wouldn't hear of staying home.

"I couldn't be with Benny when he went to be with the Lord. Nothing is going to change my mind about going to see Lacey," I said.

Upon arriving at the hospital, the staff at the front desk insisted on putting me in a wheel chair. I'm sure I must have looked like I needed admitting myself. Marilyn rolled me up to the intensive care unit where a sympathetic nurse made me a bed beside Lacey. After getting me settled, Marilyn went down to the intensive care waiting room, which was filled to overflowing. News spread in our small town of the tragedy that struck our family. It seemed that everyone—from former teachers to friends of all three of our children—was there, offering whatever help and support they could give. Everyone wanted to do something. One neighbor wanted to open a trust fund for our family, and children tried to comfort Rachel. Marilyn was gracious to them all but explained that any details would have to be handled by other family members.

"Our focus has to be on Lacey right now. We do, however, appreciate all the help."

We held Benjamin's funeral three days later. By this time, many of our family members had arrived from across the country. I can hardly express the emotions of sitting at my son's funeral, missing him terribly, yet longing to be with my daughter at the same time. It was emotionally draining. Immediately after the services, Marilyn and I headed back to the hospital to be with Lacey. As we approached her room, we noticed the surgeon Marilyn had spoken to the first night standing outside her room. His eyes were filled with tears as he turned to meet us.

"I am so sorry," he began. "I know you have been to your son's funeral. I buried my own son four years ago today. I assure you— I will do everything I can to see that your daughter survives."

We spent the majority of the next two weeks in that hospital room. Lacey was making a wonderful recovery. The neurological surgeon assigned to her told us that although they had to keep her sedated because of the respirator, he felt she had made a complete recovery from the "brain shear" she had suffered in the accident.

"I don't even think she will need much, if any, rehabilitation, which is a miracle in itself after such a severe injury."

His confident tone stemmed from the fact that Lacey was no longer heavily sedated. Whenever she was conscious, she would spell out words using sign language letters in order to ask for things. The doctor explained that signing actually took much more brain activity than talking.

"She would have to think what she wants, spell it and then sign it, which is truly remarkable."

The only problem was she kept asking about Benny. She kept signing his name over and over. The doctors had already told us that we should not tell her about her brother yet.

"She is going to want to express her feelings, and as long as she has that respirator on, she cannot talk. Her lungs are making progress. It won't be long until we can remove her from the machine. Then you can tell her, and within a few days you should be able to take her home."

We were so excited about Lacey coming home. Marilyn already had the front room set up with two hospital beds donated by a local company so that Lacey and I could recuperate together. On October 14, two weeks after we had lost Benny, the doctors told Marilyn and I to go home and get some rest.

"Tomorrow, we will take Lacey off the respirator. Get her some pictures of some friends or of the horse that she rides. She is going to need something positive to talk about with the nurses after you tell her about her brother. I believe it would be best if you were to just go home and prepare for tomorrow."

The next morning, Marilyn was busy around the house gathering up pictures and things, as the doctor had suggested, when the phone rang. It was the hospital.

"You need to come right away. Lacey has had a

massive heart attack. We have revived her, but you need to come as soon as you can."

Marilyn and I could not believe it: a heart attack. There was nothing wrong with her heart. She was a twelve-year-old girl. How could she possibly have had a heart attack?

We again found ourselves rushing to the hospital. When we arrived, the doctor met us and tried to explain what had happened. It seemed that Lacey had a rapid heartbeat due to the trauma from the accident. Before removing her from the respirator the doctors thought they needed to slow her heart rate down. Upon injecting her with a medication, she went into cardiac arrest. Instead of her heart slowing down, it stopped. They used the paddles to revive her. Unfortunately, since her lungs were still weak, the shock from the paddles caused them to have to delay removing her from the respirator. She was sedated once again, but stable. The doctors felt confident she would make a complete recovery.

The next several days were still filled with anticipation of Lacey's recovery. Sadly again, this was not the case. With Lacey's lungs being as weak as they were, they went into what is known as ARDS or adult respiratory distress syndrome. This is where the lungs begin to harden so that they can no longer hold air. The body follows in its own distress.

The days were broken up only by the terrible all-night vigils. It was wearing on all of us. In an attempt to shelter Rachel from the stress, Marilyn decided to allow her to stay with close friends in Orlando. Kim and Deago had two children her age, who had been good friends to Ben and Lacey also. After spending the weekend there, Kim was to bring Rachel to the hospital on Sunday evening so that she could go home with us and perhaps return to school. Marilyn was expecting them around 8:00 p.m., not knowing they were stuck in a traffic jam.

They were well over an hour late. I noticed that Marilyn began to fidget, constantly watching the clock. Then the unthinkable happened. They began to call out codes over the intercom in ICU. We could hear ambulances screaming into the entrance downstairs and the sound of helicopters landing on the roof. In the past, the sound of helicopters immediately took me back to Vietnam and my days as a door gunner. Now they took me to the night of the accident. Panic filled my heart, and I could see the same look on Marilyn's face. Trying to hide her concern, Marilyn rose from the chair she had been sitting in.

"I think I'll just take a walk. I need to get out of this room for a little while."

It wasn't until she entered the hall that a sigh of relief escaped from her lips. There was Rachel getting off the elevator. Marilyn and I never discussed our fears that night, but I knew that the carefree outlook we once had was forever altered.

As the days wore on, Lacey's condition worsened. The devastation caused by this condition is beyond description. Ten days after that call to return to the hospital, Lacey, swollen beyond recognition, went to be with the Lord. It was a slow, agonizing death. The doctor who had worked so hard trying to save her was devastated. He was not the one who prescribed the injection, but we could tell he was truly sorry. I saw him sit on the floor at Marilyn's feet, tears streaming down his face.

"I did everything I knew to do when the ARDS began and when her condition was deteriorating, it occurred to me that one of the top doctors in the country was visiting our hospital. I asked him to look over Lacey's chart to see if there was anything else we could do for her. I also prayed for her with a prayer group I attend. I am so sorry. I don't know what else we could have done."

When Lacey died, it was more than Marilyn could handle. I remember her letting out a cry that came from the depth of her spirit. I held on to her trembling body as she bellowed painful sobs. The peace she had experienced when Benjamin died was not there. Now there was only pain. Maybe it was the way Lacey suffered, or maybe it was the reality of all the loss crashing in on us at once, but there was no peace, no victory and no hope.

All the tragedy and loss I witnessed in war seemed to pale in comparison to witnessing the death of my own child. We buried Lacey three days later on October 28, beside her brother. Even nature itself seemed to be weeping. We had been fortunate on the day of Benjamin's funeral to be able to feel the soothing rays of the warm Florida sun. This time, a slow drizzling rain filled the air.

Even though we had Lacey's funeral on a Friday, it happened to fall on a day that was a teacher's workday, and all the children were out of school. The church was overflowing with parents and children from the community. Lacey had been a member of the Stetson University Children's Choir. There was an old Southern spiritual the choir used to sing that was Lacey's favorite song— "I'm Goin' Up a Yonder." I had asked the director, Dr. Small, if the children would mind singing it at Lacey's funeral. She had told them they could participate on a voluntary basis. As far as I could tell, most of the eighty-five children attended the funeral.

After leaving the church we held a short graveside service. Looking out from under the shelter of the small graveside canopy, I saw dozens of young girls standing in the rain, their hair soaked, the tears running harder down their cheeks than the rain flowing down their hair. Lacey's casket was covered with white roses and bright yellow sunflowers from end to end. One of Lacey's friends came up to Marilyn and asked if she could have one of the sunflowers.

"They remind me so much of Lacey, so bright and full of life," she said.

Marilyn told her she could, which started a deluge of requests.

"I would rather you girls have them to remember Lacey by than to just have them sit here on the grave and die. Would you please get one for me? Then you girls can take what you want."

We left the gravesite carrying a sunflower, but our emotions were as dark and depressed as the day.

It seemed as though Marilyn and I had come to the end of our rope. Over the past several months, we had lost our business. Because we could not pay the rent, we were being asked to vacate our home. I had lost my health, and now we had lost two of our three children. There did not seem to be one aspect of our lives that had not been devastated.

It was at this point that we began to ask ourselves the question, "Does God really love us?"

"For God so loved the world, that he gave his only begotten Son, that whosoever believeth in him should not perish, but have everlasting life."

—JOHN 3:16

7

The Question: "Does God Really Love Us?"

LOOKING BACK, I NOW SEE THAT THE LORD WAS IN the midst of our suffering, but when we were experiencing the pain of loss, we couldn't feel His presence. It seems that whenever a person is experiencing loss, whether it be the loss of a child, a spouse, a parent or even a marriage, it is the pain that numbs you to His presence as well as His voice. My brother-in-law, Stan, recently had an accident at work. He completely tore all the muscles and tendons in his shoulder and shattered the shoulder's router cuff. He was in great pain, and a co-worker later told him they were standing right in front of him, hanging on to his waist, trying to get him to sit down before he passed out.

Stan's words to me were, "The pain was so great I did not hear a word they said. I didn't even know they were there."

Well, often, that is the way it is in the spirit. The Lord is there. He has His hands on you, but all you feel is the pain. This is what we were experiencing.

It is in times like these we must trust the promises of God. It hurts. It seems like all the promises hurt, but we have to reach beyond the hurt and take God at His Word. The most important thing we have to do is settle the "love issue." No matter how we feel, we need to settle the issue of God's unending, undeserved love for us.

Although we may not understand what is happening in our lives, we have to go on with life on raw trust. We have to depend on the old cliché, "Father knows best."

There is a story starting in John 6:53 when Jesus says, "Verily, verily, I say unto you, Except ye eat the flesh of the Son of man, and drink his blood, ye have no life in you."

It goes on to say in verse 60 and 66, "Many therefore of his disciples, when they had heard this, said, 'This is a hard saying; who can hear it?' . . . From that time many of his disciples went back, and walked no more with him."

Jesus was talking, but because they could not understand what He was telling them they became offended and would not follow Him anymore. We too have a hard time understanding the ways of the Lord.

It is at this time we have to respond as Peter responded in verse 67, "Then said Jesus unto the twelve, Will ye also go away? Then Simon Peter answered him, Lord, to whom shall we go? Thou hast the words of eternal life. And we believe and are sure that thou are that Christ, the Son of the living God."

What Peter was saying was, "I don't understand. I don't know any more than the others of what you are telling us, but one thing I do know. You are the Son of God, and whether I ever understand or not, I will follow You."

That is raw trust. We may not know what the Lord is saying or what is going on when we cannot hear Him, but "to whom shall we go" but unto the Lord.

We also struggled with the thought that God must be punishing us. Although our Lord is aware of everything that happens in our lives, He is *not* the author of everything.

We have an adversary, the devil. In John 10:10, Jesus said, "The thief [the devil] cometh not, but for to steal, and to kill, and to destroy."

We have to remember that there is *no mercy* from the devil. Once he begins to destroy, he will continue. He never seems to let up. Most of all, he will try to destroy our relationship with the very one who will carry us through. In the Book of Revelations, he (the devil) is called the accuser. That is his nature. He accuses us before God and then he accuses God of things He has done.

The devil says, "If God loved you, He would not have allowed this to happen."

Please listen, God does love you, and you cannot measure God's love for you by your circumstances. God's love will become distorted if you just see it through your circumstances. *You must see God's love for you through the cross of Calvary.*

> For God so loved the world, that he gave his only begotten Son, that whosoever believeth in him should not perish, but have everlasting life.
>
> —JOHN 3:16

God, too, has experienced loss.

Romans 8:32 says, "He that spared not his own Son, but delivered him up for us all, how shall he not with him also freely give us all things?"

If you want to see God's love, just look at Calvary, at Him who spared not His own Son, even when Jesus prayed, "Abba, Father, all things are possible unto thee; take away this cup from me: nevertheless not what I will, but what thou wilt" (Mark 14:36).

Jesus asked for the cup to be taken away, yet He was still willing to do the Father's will. How hard it must have been for the Father to hear these words.

In all actuality, the Father must have thought, *"No, Jesus. I love them. You are the only one who can redeem them. You are the one who they have prophesied about through the centuries. No, Jesus. I can't spare You. I love them!"*

"He that spared not his own Son, but delivered Him up for us all" (Rom. 8:32).

Our Father knows how you feel. Jesus also knows our pain, and He loves us. Marilyn and I settled the issue of God's love for us. Do you remember that verse in Joel, "Multitudes, multitudes in the valley of decision…?"

Well, this most likely was the most crucial decision we made, to set aside all we were feeling, all that the enemy kept trying to tell us, and to say: "God loves me! I'm not perfect. There are many things I would change about my past if I could, *but God loves me!*"

Let me say it one more time. We must settle the fact that God loves us. The only place this truly can be settled once and for all is at the place called Calvary.

"For God so loved the world that he gave his only begotten son…"

I ask you how much more could He say, "I love you."

"By this shall all men know that ye are my disciples, if ye have love one to another."

—JOHN 13:35

8

The Day the Walls Came Down

THE CITY OF DeLAND, AS WELL AS MUCH OF THE greater Orlando area, was caught up in our family's story. It had been published in almost all the local newspapers, as well as broadcast on television. When Lacey died, the local newspapers carried the headline "Little Girl Joins Brother in Death."

We had lost another child, but we saw a miracle of a different sort take place. It began the day of Lacey's funeral. The church was literally overflowing with people. At least six different pastors from other local denominations were there to support us. This was not about denominational differences. It was about loving and supporting one another. Their congregations had been praying for our family, and they wanted to support us in our loss.

Immediately after the funeral the church received a call from a local foundation that had been established to help families in distress. After we returned from the funeral and reception, my brother-in-law (who returned the phone call) told us he had something important to discuss with us. He proceeded to tell us that a local foundation called and wanted to help our family. They offered to help with all of our medical bills, which by then had exceeded four hundred thousand dollars, and that they would also like to help with my needed heart transplant. There was only one problem, however. The foundation was founded by one of the area's largest alcohol distributors. Again, we found ourselves in that "valley of decision."

On the day Benjamin had died, I told Marilyn that somehow God had to be glorified, even in our loss, and that in whatever way possible we would glorify the Lord. As Marilyn and I weighed everything in the balance and recounted our decision to let God be glorified, we just could not see how He could get the glory out of alcohol money paying our bills, especially when a drunk driver had been involved in the accident. We decided to decline the money. It was after we made this decision that we saw the grace and glory of God come to work on our behalf.

All of the churches, not only in DeLand, but also in surrounding areas began to work together for our benefit. I remember a woman from the Episcopal church calling a friend of ours who attended the First Baptist Church of DeLeon Springs, which was a small town just north of us. These two congregations, along with help from others, paid the rent for one year on a lovely condominium for our family. We had been asked to move out of the house we had been living in. Although these congregations would have caught up the rent and paid any penalties, we decided we wanted to move. With my health the way it was, I spent most of my time either in bed or in our family room. Both Ben and Lacey's rooms were adjacent to the family room. After their deaths, I can remember sitting in my chair, expecting them to come out of their rooms at any moment. I would just sit and stare at their rooms, crying. Even our dog would go into Ben and Lacey's bedrooms every morning looking for them. It had been his job to wake them for school every day. So each morning he would go in searching for them. I just couldn't take it. Although we had lived in that lovely home for almost five years, we decided to move.

Many churches took up donations. Others presented the need and allowed their members to do as they felt led. There were donations from the First Assembly of God in DeLand, two local Baptist churches, the Episcopal church, the Catholic church, the First Methodist Church, the Presbyterian church and the United Church of Christ, as well as some independent congregations.

In addition to the support of the churches, there was the incredible support from the community as a whole. At the Volusia County Fair and Youth Show that year, a beef cow was put up for auction. A gentleman whose name we do not even know had purchased the cow from the 4-H Club and then put it into the auction.

He said, "You can bid on the cow, but you will not receive the meat. All the proceeds from its sale will be donated to the Rose Family Trust, and the meat will be donated to their family."

The cow was "sold" three times after the original sale. It was so successful that two hogs were also donated and sold in the same manner. In addition, a butcher volunteered to process the meat, with half of the cow and one of the hogs going directly to us. The remainder of the meat was sold at "butchered" prices, and this money was also given to us. A freezer donated by the Northwest Volusia Fern Growers was given to us to store the meat. By the time it was all said and done they had raised almost $8,000.00.

One afternoon Marilyn answered the phone, which was a rare thing for her to do. My sister, Karen, from Michigan was staying with us now, and she had a full-time job just answering the phone. But for some reason Marilyn answered this time.

Marilyn later told me, "I don't think the man expected me to answer. The first thing he said was his name and that he was the local president of the U. S. Postal Service Letter Carriers Union. When he found out that he had reached me, he began to cry."

"Oh, Mrs. Rose, we just have to do something. We are so sorry for you and your husband, and daughter. We want to help. We have taken up a collection from all the different postal workers. I need to know what to do with it."

She told him that he could deposit it into the Rose Family Trust, and he went on to say, "This is not all we plan to do. We are making up fliers to distribute to our postal customers. We are encouraging them to give to your family in the name of their postal worker. We wish we could do more."

His voice was still shaking with emotion as he said goodbye.

The children at DeLand Middle School held several car washes to raise money for our family. Plus, the children made and sold Christmas ornaments. The kids themselves also planned and held a memorial service in remembrance of Lacey and two other children who had died that year. They ended the service with the planting of three trees with a plaque marking each one.

At George Marks Elementary School in DeLand a

program called Touch a Heart was launched. Through this program, colorfully decorated containers were placed around the community to collect spare change. Also, a penny drive was instituted. Between the two projects, more than seven thousand dollars were raised in small change to benefit us and the other two girls who had been involved in the accident. It took the tellers at the bank almost a month working in their spare time to roll up the seven thousand dollars. I never knew spare change could add up to so much.

The children at the elementary school also had a memorial service for Benjamin. Several of his friends spoke, while two young boys, weeping the whole time, couldn't even hold their heads up. They too planted a tree outside Benjamin's classroom window. They all knew Benny's favorite color was red so they planted a red bottle brush tree, which has huge sweeping red blooms in the fall, and they planted a red rose bush in front of the school. The PTA purchased a marble plaque engraved with Benjamin's name and the years he lived. Benny always loved sports, so they had all his friends sign a soccer ball, which they placed in a glass case in the school library.

The DeLand Skating Center, where the children were heading on the night of the accident, held a benefit that raised almost one thousand dollars. They had hoped it would have been more, but the weather was horrible that evening, and many parents would not chance their children out in it.

Since our family's car was totaled in the accident, we were left without a vehicle. A local car dealer, Hurley Chrysler Plymouth, called us to say they wanted to donate a car. They had heard we were without a vehicle and said if Marilyn could come to their office they would like to give her one. She later told me how humbled the man seemed. Having two daughters of his own, he said he could not bear the thought of losing them, and that he and his wife wanted to help in this way. He offered her a small but very nice used Cadillac or an equally nice Volvo.

Marilyn decided on the Volvo because it had a larger trunk. She suspected I would need a wheelchair soon. It was becoming harder and harder for me to get around on my own. If I did manage to get the heart transplant, I would definitely need a wheelchair during the long and difficult recovery period.

There were donations by sororities and fraternities at Stetson University. The DeLand Cruisers car club organized a benefit car show. There were literally hundreds and hundreds of cards and letters with donations in them. They came from at least five different states. One letter even came from as far away as Germany. We didn't know the people or how they heard of our story, but many expressed their sympathy toward us and felt as if they had to help.

The local Publix grocery store set out barrels for customers to donate food, and in my hometown of Michigan, a local church also collected food and dry goods. The church, along with members of my family, had made arrangements with a local semi-truck driver to deliver the goods on his next scheduled run to Florida. They arranged for a friend of ours with a pickup to meet the driver. It was unreal—all the things they sent. We did not have to buy shampoo, deodorant, aspirin, toothpaste and other similar items for over a year.

Our garage was stuffed with food. One night a group of children from the Baptist church brought a large box of food they had collected, and without thinking Marilyn said, "Oh, kids, I thank you so much, but we really don't need any more food."

By the look on those kids' faces, you would have thought she had slapped them. I quickly intervened.

"Oh, but we do. We really do. Thank you so much."

Marilyn saw her mistake and agreed and took the box. Later she said that she would never do that again. We decided we would accept whatever anyone brought, no matter how much we had. We would then find others to give it to, and we did.

At some time during Lacey's stay at the hospital, our clothes dryer broke down. After the funeral, a friend made arrangements for a repairman to come and fix it. When Marilyn went out to see how he was doing, she found the man working on the dryer, crying his heart out. He apologized for her catching him that way and flatly refused any payment for his services.

There are too many things to mention within the scope of this book. Truly, I could write page after page. In the end, we knew we had experienced what the grace of God can do when the church and community walls come down and everyone works together.

We had filed the paperwork on my disability before the children's accident, so I was declared disabled. Medicare stepped in and picked up the majority of the hospital bills. The remainder of all the bills were paid through the Rose Family Trust, and there was enough money for us to live comfortably for over a year. Every bill was paid, and the Lord gave us a time to heal.

Approximately a week after Lacey's death, I finally

made it to Shands Hospital at the University of Florida for the evaluation of whether I would be eligible for a transplant. After an extensive physical, as well as mental, examination, they came to the grim conclusion.

"Mr. Rose, we are sorry but after extensive testing, we have determined that your psychological profile will not allow us to put you on our waiting list. The short of it, you are grieving the loss of your children and are extremely depressed. To survive an operation the magnitude of a heart transplant you have to be prepared mentally and have a strong will to live. We believe you have neither at the present time. A heart is a very precious commodity. We can only accept those candidates we feel have the greatest chance of survival. We will, however, monitor your progress. If we find you are improving in this area, we will take another look at your case."

It was yet another grim prognosis. By this time, bad news had lost its shock value for Marilyn and I. We both seemed to accept the decision without much reservation. Since I was without insurance, they decided to enroll me in a drug study program, where some of the patients take an experimental drug while the other patients take placebos. Not even the nursing staff knows who gets what, but on this program they monitor your health very carefully at the expense of the drug companies. At first they put me on a very vigorous schedule with three appointments a week. Then I was moved to once a week and finally, once a month.

However, neither my physical or psychological profile was getting any better. In fact, I was falling into deeper and deeper depression. The holiday season was quickly approaching. With both

Benjamin and Lacey's birthdays falling in December, we were not looking forward to what once seemed to be a month of celebrations.

The hopelessness of my condition and the advice from my doctors to get my affairs in order hung heavy over my head. Marilyn and I decided that there just wasn't anything we wanted to get each other for Christmas. We had done some shopping for Rachel, but there wasn't anything we wanted. I had become so discouraged that several days before Christmas I asked Marilyn to take me out to the cemetery. There was something I wanted to do. She drove me out thinking I wanted to go to the children's grave. To her surprise, I told her I wanted to stop in the office. She parked the car and we went inside. I told the employees I had come to buy my grave and make the necessary arrangements. Marilyn made little response as I proceeded to pick out two sites just up the hill from the kids. The cemetery didn't have any plots available right beside the children, but they did have "two lovely spots" just up the hill. That was basically the extent of our Christmas shopping for one another: no packages, no bows, just two graves on the hill.

"They that wait upon the Lord shall renew their strength; they shall mount up with wings as eagles; they shall run, and not be weary; and they shall walk, and not faint."

—ISAIAH 40:31

9

Waiting on the Lord

ARILYN, ON THE OTHER HAND, WAS DOING HER best to hold things together. Rachel was having a terrible time trying to adjust to being an only child. All of her life she had been the baby of the family and had grown accustomed to having an older brother and sister, whom she depended upon. The majority of her activities had revolved around them and their friends. Death had become a reality to this eight-year-old child.

My daughter, who just weeks ago had been unable to leave my side, now began to separate herself from me. In her little mind, she was afraid I too was going to die. In her great pain, she became more and more distant toward me. It was not because she did not love me. In fact, it was because of her love for me. This was so hard to understand. Just when I needed a child to hold, she withdrew and became distant.

Marilyn, in an attempt to get her some sort of help, decided to take her to a group headed by Hospice for grieving children. Rachel would have nothing to do with it unless Marilyn was going to go to a group, too. So Marilyn found an adult group meeting across the street at the same time a children's group met. She felt that the meetings might give Rachel an opportunity to express some of the feelings she was obviously suppressing. Rachel suppressed her feelings so deeply that she wouldn't even mention either her brother's or sister's name. Marilyn had discovered pictures of them hidden in her pillow case and had also found Benjamin's "treasure chest," as he called it, under her bed. But Rachel would not talk about them at all.

Unfortunately, Rachel did not seem to benefit from the group. Hospice told us she just wasn't ready to deal with it. Every time they would try to get her involved in a conversation, she would either not answer or give them an answer to cut the conversation short. To Marilyn's surprise, however, she found her group quite beneficial, especially the final assignment they asked them to do. At the end of the four-week session, they wanted each person to draw something, write a poem or do a dance to express how they felt at three different stages in their lives:

1. How they felt before they lost their loved one;
2. How they felt now;
3. How they saw themselves in the future.

Let me allow Marilyn to explain what she did in her own words:

MARILYN'S DRAWING

I (Marilyn) like to draw, so I decided I was going to

draw a picture. I got a large posterboard and some colored pencils and began to draw. I began by drawing a large heart. This heart was broken into three sections. In the first section, or the upper-left-hand part of the heart, I drew a vessel with five flowers in it. When I explained my drawing to the class, I told them that the vessel holding the flowers was my life. Like the vessel, my life was full and beautiful. Each flower represented a member of our family.

There was a rose for my husband, Tom, for our last name, Rose, and a rose bud for our son, Benjamin. I drew a sunflower for Lacey. She loved sunflowers. We even buried her with one in her hair. Our Rachel reminded me of a daisy. She was always so happy and carefree. Last of all, I had myself as a stem of sweet peas because Tom used to call me "Sweet Pea" when we were dating.

In the second section of the heart, which was the bottom portion, the vessel was shattered and broken. Two of the flowers, the rose bud and the sunflower, were dead, and the rose was almost dead. Finally, the last two flowers, the daisy and the sweet peas, were lying wilting away. I told the class that this was my life now. Two of my children were gone, my husband was barely hanging on to life, and I felt like Rachel and I were wasting away.

Then, in the upper-right-hand corner of the heart, I drew the vessel as closely as I could to the first time— only it had two jagged holes in the side of it. I took a yellow pencil and colored the inside of these holes as brightly as I could. The three flowers—the rose, the daisy and the sweet peas—were alive and healthy again. I also drew a soaring eagle over the vessel with Isaiah 40:31 written under it. I explained to my class that this is how I saw my life in the future.

"They that wait upon the Lord shall renew their strength; they shall mount up with wings as eagles; they shall run, and not be weary; and they shall walk, and not faint."

I told them I believed that the Lord was going to put my life back together again. The two holes in the side of the vessel represented my two children that were gone. Nothing could ever replace them. I will always bear the scars of losing them, but the bright yellow is the glory of the Lord. I have asked the Lord not only to put my life back together again, but that the Spirit of the Lord would fill in the areas where the enemy had wounded me so that God's glory would shine forth and touch others' lives. This is what I pray, and this is how I see my life in the future.

It was some time later that I discovered two passages from the Book of Isaiah that confirmed this. Isaiah 31:4 says,

> This is what the Lord says to me, "As a lion growls, a great lion over his prey—and though a whole band of shepherds is called together against him, he is not frightened by their shouts or disturbed by their clamor"—so the Lord Almighty will come down to do battle on Mount Zion and on its heights.
>
> —NIV

Now when I read this, I am reminded that Jesus told us the devil goes about as a roaring lion. We often hear the lion roar in our lives. When the doctor tells you your husband has heart disease or cancer, you hear the roar. Maybe they are talking lay-offs at work. In all of these things, we hear the roar of the lion, but we need to remember that his roar does not frighten the Lord, and neither is He disturbed by his clamor, but He will come down and fight for us. Run to the Lord and allow Him to fight your battles.

"The battle is mine, *not* yours, saith the Lord."

That's why David said,

> "The LORD is my rock, and my fortress, and my deliverer; my God, my strength, in whom I will trust . . ."
>
> —PSALM 18:2

Remember our verse: "Multitudes, multitudes in the valley of decision: for the day of the Lord is near in the valley of decision. The sun and the moon shall be darkened, and the stars shall withdraw their shining. The Lord also shall roar out of Zion, and utter his voice from Jerusalem; and the heavens and the earth shall shake: but the Lord will be the hope of his people, and the strength of the children of Israel" (Joel 3:14-16). The Lord is our hope!

What if the devil is already in the camp? What if he has already destroyed? This is what happened in our lives. Well, we still need to run to the Lord, to Mount Zion.

Isaiah 51:3 says, "For the Lord shall comfort Zion: he will comfort all her waste places; and he will make her wilderness like Eden, and her desert like the garden of the Lord; joy and gladness shall be found therein, thanksgiving, and the voice of melody."

Isaiah goes on to say, "Therefore the redeemed of the Lord shall return, and come with singing unto Zion; and everlasting joy shall be upon their head: they shall obtain gladness and joy; and sorrow and mourning shall flee away" (Is. 51:11).

When I found this verse, I knew that not only does the Lord come down to fight for us out of Zion, but that He will also restore us. If we never had waste places, there would be no need for Him to make them like the Garden of the Lord. God not only restores, but He also makes us better and stronger than before if we will allow Him. He is a God of new creations. Old things pass away, and behold all things become new.

The very verse that Jesus quoted in Luke 4:18–19 about Himself is found in Isaiah 61:

> The spirit of the Lord God is upon me; because the Lord hath anointed me to preach good tidings unto the meek; he hath sent me to bind up the brokenhearted, to proclaim liberty to the captives, and the opening of the prison to them that are bound;
>
> To proclaim the acceptable year of the Lord, and the day of vengeance of our God; to comfort all that mourn;
>
> To appoint unto them that mourn in Zion, to give unto them beauty for ashes, the oil of joy for mourning, the garment of praise for the spirit of heaviness; that they might be called trees of righteousness, the planting of the Lord, that he might be glorified.

Jesus said he would bind up the brokenhearted. It is not an instant healing. The *American Heritage Dictionary* defines the word *bind* as "to wrap up by encircling." That is just what Jesus does, if we will allow Him. He wraps us up in His love and encircles

us until we have had time to heal. Then we may
return to Zion, "and come with singing unto Zion;
and everlasting joy shall be upon their head: they
shall obtain gladness and joy; and sorrow and
mourning shall flee away" (Is. 51:11).

"But I would not have you to be ignorant, brethren, concerning them which are asleep, that ye sorrow not, even as others which have no hope."

— 1 Thessalonians 4:13

10

Do Not Sorrow

A S WINTER GAVE WAY TO SPRINGTIME, I (TOM) WAS not getting any better. It seemed like all I did was cry. I couldn't work. I didn't have the strength to do much of anything. Marilyn, Rachel and I did, however, continue to go to church. We would pull up and park in the handicapped parking, and Marilyn would help me into the church, where the ushers would help me to my seat. As I have said before, all the promises seemed to hurt. The praise and worship hurt. There wasn't any part of the service that I really enjoyed, yet I knew I needed to stay under the anointing. I needed to stay in the body of Christ no matter how I felt.

God knew how I felt, and He knows how you feel. There is no point in trying to hide it. I am often asked if I was mad at God during this time. I really can't say that I was. I think I was too weak to be mad. I just didn't have any fight left in me, but for those of you who do struggle with being angry with God: *it is OK*. Your Father knows how you feel. He also knows that anger is a natural reaction to pain.

When Marilyn and I were first married, we had this young, sweet dog. She was quite docile, and she loved both of us. One night she got out on the country road where we lived and was struck by a car. As she lay in the road, I ran to help her. She had broken her hip and was in terrible pain. As I reached down to move her, all of a sudden she lashed out and bit my hand severely, to the point that I needed stitches. It wasn't that she didn't love me, because she did. She was reacting to the pain.

Unfortunately, it is not only dogs who "bite" when they experience pain. People do too, and they normally bite the ones who are closest to them, the ones they love.

I didn't blame our dog for biting me. I could see how much pain she was in. I picked her up, willing to suffer being bitten again and again because I loved her, a dog. How much more will your heavenly Father suffer you biting at Him? He has great big shoulders, and He loves you. I didn't leave my dog in the road because she bit me, and your heavenly Father won't leave you because you have lashed out in the midst of your pain. You don't need to repress how you feel. Your Father knows anyway. If you are angry, tell Him.

"If we confess our sins [including anger], He is faithful and just to forgive us our sins, and to cleanse us from all unrighteousness" (1 John 1:9).

If we confess the sin, He will open the door for His Spirit to come in and change us, to heal the hurt that is causing the anger. Don't expect to change instantaneously. The pain is too great, but He will forgive and He will heal us if we will allow Him.

The spring did not seem to hold any hope for me. I remember one day in particular when I was feeling especially low. Marilyn and Rachel had an appointment, and they were getting ready to leave the house. I came out of my room to tell them goodbye.

Rachel had already gone outside when I looked at Marilyn, "I can't take it anymore, Marilyn. I have asked the Lord to take me home. I can't stand just sitting around the house crying. I can't work. I have no strength to go out. All I do is cry."

I don't know what kind of response I was looking for, but I wasn't expecting Marilyn to say in a tone that was almost angry, "Tom, don't you leave me. Rachel and I have already lost too much. We don't need to lose you, too. Don't you give up, Tom. We need you. Don't you give up."

Having said that, she left. After watching them disappear down the sidewalk to the car, I went down to sit in my big green chair, thinking, *This is all I do. I go from the bed to the chair and then back to the bed.*

As I sat there that afternoon I began to talk with the Lord, "Lord, I know You love me. I have settled that in my heart, but if You do not heal me, I'm asking You to take me home. I just can't live like this any longer."

As I sat there weak, depressed and talking to the Lord, I don't know whether I fell asleep or if I was awake. I really couldn't tell, but Jesus appeared there in our living room. As He stood there, He opened His arms, and my daughter Lacey appeared on His right side. She stood there smiling at me with her eyes flashing in that same way her Mama used to smile at me and make my heart leap. Then Benjamin appeared on His left side. Benjamin's lips weren't moving, yet I could hear him speak.

"Papa, do you really believe all those Bible stories you read to us? Do you really believe in a place called heaven, Papa? Do you really believe in the gift of eternal life?"

I heard all these questions in his tender little voice.

"Papa, do you remember what you used to tell me about my school work or my karate lessons or my riding lessons—how I was to focus and to finish everything I started? Papa, focus. You have to focus on Jesus. Don't come across the finish line all broken in body and spirit. Focus on Jesus and finish strong. He has a work for you to do if you will focus and finish strong."

That was it, and they were gone as quickly as they had come.

When Marilyn and Rachel returned home that evening, I met them at the door. For the first time in months, a ray of hope had entered my life. "Marilyn, I've seen Jesus; I've seen the kids. I really think maybe things are going to work out."

I can't say I was full of joy or of faith for the future, but hope had returned, and sometimes hope is enough—just a glimmer of hope. The next morning was Sunday. It was time to go to church. You would have thought I would have been excited to go. Maybe it was still the weakness of my physical condition. Maybe it was doubt trying to creep in. I don't know. All I know is that I didn't feel the glimmer of hope I had just experienced the night before. Did I really see them? Did Jesus really appear? Maybe it was my mind playing tricks on me. The questions kept running through my head. Yet, off to church we went. We parked in the handicapped parking, as usual. The ushers helped me to my accustomed seat. I had my own seat, you know, as do many of you, I'm sure. I sat there as the choir and the praise and worship team began to lift up the name of Jesus. Marilyn was on her feet, hands raised, praising the Lord. Marilyn continually praised the Lord.

Whenever she was asked about it she would explain, "I don't know. Maybe you could call it a revenge thing. It's not that I am so strong or that I have a great faith. Really, I have little faith in a great big God. That is all He asks of us—to have the faith of a mustard seed. In the beginning I worshiped out of revenge toward the devil. One thing I had learned early on in my Christian life was the devil hates to hear the praises of our God. I was so angry with the devil that I wished I could hurt him. If only I could get my hands on him, but I couldn't. I could however, praise the Lord.

"I remember thinking one day, *Devil, we had to move out of our home. You stole my children, you took the health of my husband, but there is one thing you cannot take—that is my praise. As long as I have a breath left in my body, I will praise the Lord. I know how you hate the praises of our Lord; therefore, I will praise the Lord.*

"Was this a right way to think? I don't know. Truly God deserves our praises because of who He is. My motives were not right. Yet God in all His mercy is not looking for ways to condemn us. He is looking for a way to bless us and heal us. He wants to help us in our time of need. So often we feel like God loves us at the moment we are saved. From that point on we think we disappoint Him and continue to make Him mad with every wrong motive and every wrong action.

"Yet, Jesus Himself said, 'For God sent not his Son into the world to condemn the world; but that the world through him might be saved,' (John 3:17).

"Were my motives wrong? Perhaps, but I truly believe God says, 'I can work with that. The motives might be off, but I can work with that.'

"Little by little, the Lord began to heal my broken and bruised spirit. I no longer have to praise the Lord out of revenge toward the devil, but I praise Him because He has bound up my broken heart. He has given unto me beauty for ashes, the oil of joy for mourning, the garment of praise for the spirit of heaviness."

So Marilyn was standing there in church, praising the Lord. Although she was praising the Lord, she often wept, too. I sat there in my seat, crying as usual. I looked up at Marilyn; tears had been streaming down her face. Black circles of mascara made her look like a little raccoon from rubbing her eyes so much.

I continued to sit there, bent over and crying. When the Spirit of the Lord spoke to me. It was not an audible voice, but it was as clear as if it had been:

"If you will stand up and praise me, *today* I will heal you."

I just sat there, caught in the valley of decision. Did I want to stand up? Did I even want to be healed? It would be easier to just go home and be with the Lord, Ben and Lacey. I was tired—tired of being sick, tired of being sad. Even if I were healed, that wouldn't bring Ben and Lacey back to me.

With all those thoughts, I remembered what Marilyn had said the day before, "Don't you leave us. Rachel and I have lost too much already. We need you. Don't you leave us."

Then came the words Benjamin spoke in the vision, "Do you believe? Focus, Papa. Focus on Jesus and finish strong. Don't come across the finish line all broken in spirit. Jesus has a work for you to do if you will focus, Papa."

As I sat there the Spirit of the Lord spoke to me one more time, "If you will stand up and praise me, *today* I will heal you."

The Lord always leaves the decision to us. I could stand up and begin to praise Him, or I could sit there and die. Maybe not die right then—but if the heart disease didn't get me, the broken heart surely would have. I pushed my cane aside, grabbed hold of the pew in front of me, and pulled myself to my feet. As I stood there all wobbly-legged, I lifted my hands and began to thank and praise the Lord.

"Oh, Lord, I don't understand everything that has happened in my life, but I love You, Lord, and I praise You. I thank You for all the good years You gave to me. I thank You for the three beautiful babies and how You caused us to prosper, but most of all I thank You for what You did that day for me at Calvary. I praise You for the free gift of eternal life."

As I stood there and offered up a sacrifice of praise, the Spirit of the Lord came upon me. Now, this strong 200-pound man had become a 160-pound weakling with a heart working at fifteen percent capacity and a weak body from months of lying around in bed. It is no small thing when the Spirit of the Lord comes upon you. I remember leaning against the pew in front of me with my whole body trembling. Marilyn grabbed my arm.

With a look of alarm, she asked, "Are you all right?"

I think she thought I was going home to heaven right there in church. Having the big one—a heart attack.

I told her, "I'm OK. It is the Lord. The Spirit of the Lord is on me."

Now Marilyn and I have been Pentecostals for some seventeen years. In most Pentecostal circles, when the Spirit of God comes upon you, you either take off running or dancing or you give a message. Well, Marilyn knew it wasn't like me to run, and I surely wasn't going to take off dancing in my condition.

So she said, "Well, just give the message."

Still sounding a little frantic, I said to Marilyn, "You don't understand. It's not like that. I don't have a message. I haven't ever felt anything like this."

As I stood there shaking, I could feel my heart getting hot. I grabbed the side of my chest and bent over, trying to catch my breath. My chest kept getting hotter and hotter. By now I was completely bent over from the waist with my heart feeling as if it were on fire.

I remember saying, in my mind I think, *Lord, what are You doing to me?*

Immediately the answer came, "This is My resurrection power."

It is the same power that raised Jesus from the dead. It is that same power that will raise us up on that last day. It dwells in each and every one of us. Praise God! He has placed in each and every one of us that resurrection power.

Finally, the trembling and heat diminished. I sat down, still stunned from it all. I wish I could say that I got up and ran around the church, that I jumped to my feet completely healed, but I didn't. I walked out of the church that day almost the same as I walked in. However, one thing had changed. I had an encounter with the living God. I knew He had touched me. I began to thank Him every day.

Each morning, I got out of bed and said, "Lord, I

thank You for what You did that day at the DeLand
Sanctuary Church of God. I praise You, Lord, for
healing my body."

Day by day, little by little, I began to get better. At
first, I just felt better, but the doctors kept telling me
my physical condition had not changed. Still, I could
feel my body growing stronger and stronger. As the
weeks stretched into months, my progress continued. It was during this time that Rachel, Marilyn
and myself went to spend some time in Colorado.
The doctors thought it would be good for me to get
out of the heat and humidity of our Florida summers.
The cool, dry conditions of Colorado would be ideal,
as long as I stayed out of the higher altitudes.

Marilyn and I both have family living there as well
as friends, so we decided to make the trip. I really
believe the Lord gave us this time not only for me to
begin to heal physically, but also for all of us to
bond again as a family. We were different. None of
us would ever be the same. I think change is resisted
by some people who have lost loved ones. They
want things to be the same, but they never will be.
That doesn't mean we can't be happy, but we have
to accept the fact that each of us are different.

The day Lacey died, Lacey's doctor, a Christian
who had also lost a son just four years prior to our
loss, took Marilyn and I aside and gave us wonderful
advice.

He said, "Now you two are going to have to give
each other space to grieve because men and women
do not grieve the same. One may want to talk while
the other one does not. This is OK. Don't try to
make your spouse feel the same way you do. Just
because your spouse doesn't express it in the same
fashion does not mean that he or she loved the one

who has died less. It does not mean that at all. Each person deals with it in another way."

He went on to tell us, "Almost seventy-five percent of marriages that lose a child end in divorce. This does not need to happen—just allow each other space and don't be quick to judge each other's feelings."

So in Colorado the Lord began not only the physical healing process, but He also began to bind up our broken hearts and bind us together again as a family. Some of the days were rough. There were travel days out on the open road where we sat silently driving, tears falling like rain from our eyes, yet the healing process was beginning.

We spent most of that first summer out in Colorado. I was still very weak, but each day I would get up and thank the Lord for healing my body. By the end of the summer, I not only went up into the higher elevations of the Colorado mountains, but I actually did a little bit of hiking. It was nothing strenuous, but just being out there in the cool, fresh air seemed to make a world of difference. There is something about the grandeur of those mountains that makes you feel closer to the Lord.

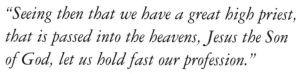

"Seeing then that we have a great high priest, that is passed into the heavens, Jesus the Son of God, let us hold fast our profession."

—HEBREWS 4:14

11

Hold Fast Your Profession

U PON OUR RETURN HOME, I BEGAN THE CIRCLE OF examinations. I started with my local doctor. I had three doctors that I saw regularly. On that first appointment after our return home, I was enthusiastic about the way I was feeling.

"Hey, Doc. I'm doing better. I know I am."

The doctor examined me and said, "I don't think so. In fact, I don't like the way your lungs sound. They sound like they might be filling up with fluid again."

I told him I didn't think so, that I felt much better, and that while I was out in Colorado I had gotten some of my strength back. He decided he would let me go for another couple of weeks.

"…But I want to see you in two weeks. If your lungs don't sound any better, I want to run some tests."

I agreed and returned on the requested day. He still thought I did not sound good and decided to order an echocardiogram.

The devil always wants you to believe the bad report. He will even use good people to try to discourage you, but you have to hang on to God. Hang on to your confession. It is a powerful weapon. "(For the weapons of our warfare are not carnal, but mighty through God to the pulling down of strongholds;) casting down imaginations, and every high thing that exalteth itself against the knowledge of God, and bringing into captivity every thought to the obedience of Christ" (2 Cor. 10:4–5).

We must focus on Jesus and what He has done for us.

Revelation 12:11a tells us, "And they overcame him [the devil] by the blood of the Lamb, and by the word of their testimony."

Our confession is vital.

Paul says in Hebrews 4:14–16, "Seeing then that we have a great high priest, that is passed into the heavens, Jesus the Son of God, let us hold fast our profession. For we have not a high priest which cannot be touched with the feeling of our infirmities; but was in all points tempted as we are, yet without sin. Let us therefore come boldly unto the throne of grace, that we my obtain mercy, and find grace to help in time of need."

We have a High Priest who stands at the right hand of the Father, ever making intercession for us. Paul tells us to hold fast our profession. Now the Greek word here is *homologia*, which is also translated as "confession." Paul says since we have a great High Priest, Jesus, ever making intercession for us, we need to hold fast our confession. This is very important because Jesus tells us whatever we confess before men, He will confess before the Father. We often feel that He was only talking about confessing Him as Lord (and He was talking about that), but it is also true of our confession in general.

If we come to a meeting, and we feel the power of

God go through our bodies and we say, "Praise the Lord! I'm healed!" then Jesus, acting as our high priest, says, "Father, he is saying he is healed." We then go home and begin to feel the pain again, so we say, "Well, I guess I didn't get it. I guess I am not healed." A priest can only confess what you confess, so Jesus says, "Father, he is saying he is not healed," and on and on it goes.

This is why James tells us, "Let him ask in faith, *nothing wavering*. For he that wavereth is like a wave of the sea driven with the wind and tossed. For let not that man think that he shall receive any thing of the Lord" (James 1:6–7, italics added).

It is not that the Lord does not love you. He does very much, but He is our High Priest, and He must confess what we confess. There were several times when the pain would well up in my chest. Sweat would bead up on my forehead.

When this would happen, I would immediately jump to my feet and say, "You lying devil (casting down imaginations, and every high thing that exalteth itself against the knowledge of God), God healed me that day at the DeLand Sanctuary Church!" I would confess the time and place that Jesus healed me. Then I kept standing (which often took all my strength and will power), and I praised the Lord.

As the doctor ordered, I had the echocardiogram done. Of course, when they had finished administering the test, the technicians could not tell me the results. I would have to wait until the doctor had a chance to read them. As I waited, I continued to praise the Lord.

"O praise the Lord, all ye nations: praise him, all ye people. For his merciful kindness is great toward us: and the truth of the Lord endureth for ever. Praise ye the Lord."

—PSALM 117

12

Why Praise Him?

I HAVE OFTEN WONDERED WHY THE LORD HAD ME praise Him in the church. Why didn't He just heal me? At the time it was all happening, I didn't realize all that was going on in the spirit.

When I stood up that morning, I first began to thank the Lord. Sometimes, when we are unable to praise the Lord, when there just is not praise in our spirits, we can start by giving thanks. This is where we start; giving thanks is a way of getting the wheels of our faith moving.

David said, "Enter into his gates with thanksgiving" (Ps. 100:4).

Thanksgiving is a starting place for our spirits. It sets up markers for us to see what God has already done on our behalf. When God gave the children of Israel a victory over the enemy, they set up a pillar to remember what the Lord had done for them. That is what thanksgiving does. It goes back over the pillars of victory God has already done in our lives. We all have pillars of victory. If we have been saved, we have a pillar. The Lord has revealed Himself as a pillar of strength to those in need throughout the Scriptures. To Shadrach, Meshach and Abednego, He was the fourth man in the midst of the burning fiery furnace. To Nehemiah, He was the rebuilder of broken dreams and broken lives. To Nahum, He was a stronghold in a day of trouble.

Therefore, Paul tells us, "In everything give thanks."

This is often misunderstood. Paul did not say *for* everything give thanks. We are not instructed to give thanks *for* everything that happens to us. As I said before, God is not the author of everything that happens in our lives, but if we will give thanks *in* everything, the wheels of faith will begin turning in our spirits. As I was giving thanks, faith came alive in my spirit, and then I could praise the Lord. Once my spirit moved into praise, the Spirit of the Lord moved on me.

I believe there are several reasons God requires praise. The first and foremost is that *praise changes our focus.* Benjamin said to me, "Papa, *focus* on Jesus." When we praise the Lord, we are encouraged by the Holy Spirit to turn away from ourselves, from all the hurt, the pain, the anger, from our situation, whatever it might be. Then, the words of our mouths cause us to focus on the one about whom we are testifying (Remember, we will overcome the devil by our testimony). As we begin to speak of God's goodness, of His grace, of His works, of His faithfulness, and of His love, our attention is taken off our problems and placed on the problem solver. The more we speak of Him, the clearer He becomes. He becomes brighter and brighter, until His brightness overtakes the darkness of our lives.

That is why Hebrews 12:2 says, "Looking unto

Jesus the author and finisher of our faith..."

As we focus on Him (looking unto Him), faith will arise in our spirits. His words become alive and are life to us.

This is why David said, "This is my comfort in my affliction: for thy word hath quickened me," (Ps. 119:50).

The Hebrew word for quickened means "to revive, recover, restore." As we speak of His goodness and focus on His person, our spirit opens up so that He can pour His grace into us, for all of His promises are hinged on His grace, *not on us.* They hinge on what He did for us that day at Calvary.

When the Holy Spirit prompted me to say, "But most of all I thank You and praise You, Lord, for what You did for me (it became very personal) *that day on calvary,*" I did not realize the magnitude of what I was saying. All His promises hinge on that fact.

When Jesus says, "Your sins are forgiven... Go in peace," or, "Arise and be healed," or, "Take up thy bed and walk," they are all hinged on what He did for us *that day on calvary.* My focus was not on my problem. I was not pleading with Him to deliver me out of my problems. I was focused on Him, and through the praises for what *He* had done for *me* at Calvary, I was exposed to His mercy and His grace, "For his mercy endures forever" (Ps. 136).

Peter could walk on water as long as his focus stayed on Jesus. He only began to sink when his eyes were off Jesus and onto the waves that wanted to overflow him. Stephen, on trial for his life, focused on Jesus until his face glowed with the glory of God like an angel. The more they persecuted him, the more Stephen focused. Jesus became brighter and brighter until Stephen looking up "saw the glory of God, and Jesus standing on the right hand of God" (Acts 7:55). When your circumstances want to overflow you, "focus on Jesus." Praise God; focus.

The second thing praise does is drive back the forces of darkness.

Psalm 22:3 tells us, "But thou art holy, O thou that inhabitest the praises of Israel."

God inhabits or lives in the praises of His people. God is light, and in Him there is no darkness. When the Spirit of the Lord moves in, the enemy is scattered.

David said, "Let God arise [Let Him arise and inhabit your praise], let his enemies be scattered" (Ps. 68:1).

The third thing praise does is this: God changes our garment through our praises. Isaiah 61:3, speaking of Jesus, says that He will give us "the garment of praise for the spirit of heaviness."

As we praise the Lord, that spirit of heaviness is lifted, maybe only for a moment at first. But as we continue to praise Him we will find ourselves clothed in a brand-new garment, "that we might be called the trees of righteousness, the planting of the Lord, that He might be glorified" (Is. 61:3).

"Oh praise the Lord, all ye nations: praise him, all ye people. For his merciful kindness is great toward us: and the truth of the Lord endureth for ever. Praise ye the Lord" (Ps. 117).

After having the echocardiogram, it was several days before I got the results. Rachel, Marilyn and I had just returned from church on a Sunday night when the phone rang. It was my local doctor on the other end of the line.

"Mr. Rose, I was just reading your echo, and I had

to call you. *You are better.* I do not have the exact reading to tell you how much better, but in comparing your last echo with this one it is obvious that you are much better."

He was so excited! Have you ever heard of doctor calling at 9:30 on a Sunday night to deliver good news? I hadn't until then, but it was a miracle in progress. The following week, I went to Orlando to the heart specialist. He had received a copy of the echocardiogram from my local doctor. When I got there, I did a little two-step into the waiting room and hopped up on the table. The nurse let out a slight giggle at my enthusiasm. (Keep in mind that I was going to see the same doctor who gave me, "the grim prognosis" the day they sent me home to wait for for a heart transplant.) When the doctor came in the room, he plopped down in a chair, with a look of wonder on his face.

"Mr. Rose, I read your echo, and seeing how you look today is truly remarkable. To tell you the truth, I would have given you about a million to one odds that you would not have made it, considering the amount of stress you have experienced over the past several months."

This was also the doctor who gave Marilyn advice on how to break the news to me about Benjamin. I looked the doctor straight in the eye, not trying to be obnoxious, but knowing in whom I believe, I said:

"Yeah, Doc, but I know the *One*."

It doesn't matter how the odds are stacked against you, as long as you have just One on your side, and that One is Jesus, you can overcome all the rest.

Shands Hospital was the last to recognize the fact that I had gotten better. They started out by calling it a "spontaneous recovery." I continually told them that it wasn't just spontaneous. The fact of the matter was that Jesus had healed me. They finally caved in and added, "spontaneous recovery due to a higher power." Well, I guess that was better than nothing. They may not know His name, but at least they have one thing right: He is a much higher power. In fact, there is none like Him.

"For if ye forgive men their trespasses, your heavenly Father will also forgive you: but if ye forgive not men their trespasses, neither will your Father forgive your trespasses."

—MATTHEW 6:14–15

13

Forgiveness:
It's a Choice, Not a Feeling

I**T TOOK OVER A YEAR FOR THE DOCTORS TO CAUTIOUSLY** agree that something miraculous had happened in my life. However, there is one key that I have not mentioned. That is, Marilyn and I chose to forgive. We found ourselves once again in the valley of decision. We chose to forgive a drunk driver, and a mistake made at a hospital, and decided we would not sue, even when there were lawyers that would have loved to take the case. We made the choice and decided that we must forgive.

Isaiah 55:7 says, "Let the wicked forsake his way, and the unrighteous man his thoughts: and let him return unto the Lord, and he will have mercy upon him; and to our God, for he will abundantly pardon."

After the accident, I had a hard time forgiving the drunk driver who was involved. The man was found guilty in a court of law and was given a jail sentence. Yet the Bible tells us we must forgive.

Jesus taught us in Matthew 6:14, "For if ye forgive

men their trespasses, your heavenly Father will also forgive you: but if ye forgive not men their trespasses, neither will your Father forgive your trespasses."

That's a strong statement. Jesus does not say it would be nice if we forgave or we would be better off if we forgave. He said we *must* forgive. It is a command, and every command becomes a choice. Here, the valley of decision comes into play again. Many people make the mistake of thinking that forgiveness is a feeling. Forgiveness is not a feeling; it is a choice! You might say, "Well, that sounds good, but how do I do that?"

Remember the verse from Isaiah that said let the unrighteous man forsake his thoughts? This verse tells us that we have to choose to lay it down. Every time we replay the offense over in our minds we must say to ourselves, "I have chosen to forgive this person. I will not think about this any longer. They are forgiven." At first this is hard. We have to forsake thoughts of resentment, anger, retaliation or unrighteous actions, and we have to choose to forgive. We should force our minds (we take every thought captive) to think on something else.

"Casting down imaginations, and every high thing that exalteth itself against the knowledge of God [or God's will], and bringing into captivity every thought to the obedience of Christ" (2 Cor. 10:5).

"Finally, brethren, whatsoever things are true, whatsoever things are honest, whatsoever things are just, whatsoever things are pure, whatsoever things are of good report; if there be any virtue, and if there be any praise, think on these things" (Phil. 4:8).

If you will think as God commands, the feelings will come. They come supernaturally. They come from Calvary. You choose to forgive, and God does the work. Remember, forgiveness is not a feeling. The feelings come *after* the forgiveness. You must choose to forsake the thoughts and forgive the person, and God will do the rest.

Just as I confessed my healing, I also confessed that I had forgiven the drunk driver. At first, I did it just because Marilyn would not leave me alone.

She continued to say, "Tom, you must forgive."

So I would say with an attitude, "OK! I forgive!"

Each day I would confess the fact that I had forgiven the man. Little by little, as I forsook the thoughts and chose to forgive, the feelings came. It starts in the mind, but it changes the heart.

There is something else I want to share with you about forgiving. When we choose to forgive and we walk in that forgiveness, it never fails that someone will remind you of the offense or something will happen that causes all the unrighteous feelings to flood your soul. Suddenly, there he is, the accuser of your soul, the devil.

He will say, "See, I knew you had not forgiven. You just thought you had."

At this point you need to say, "You lying devil, I have forgiven. I have chosen to forgive, and I have forgiven."

The devil does not want you to forgive because unforgiveness is a bigger hindrance to us than any other obstacle. You need to rebuke him in the name of Jesus. Remember this: it takes God to tear down the walls of unforgiveness in our lives, and, to paraphrase Joshua, "Cursed be the man who rebuilds that which God has torn down."

REGRET

Don't let the devil rebuild those walls of unforgiveness. He will try, but if you stand firm, he cannot rebuild them. For many of us, unforgiveness is bigger then we are. We cannot do it in our own strength. That strength must come from Calvary. However, for some, the hardest people to forgive are themselves. Many of us, after experiencing a tragedy, find ourselves living in the land of "should have, could have and would have," on a street called "if only."

We tell ourselves, "If only I had known, I could have done this. If only I had known, I could have done that."

When we find ourselves or a loved one living there, we need to take another trip to Calvary. We all have regrets. There are things in each of our lives we could have done differently, but as Paul says, "But this one thing I do, forgetting those things which are behind, and reaching forth unto those things which are before, I press toward the mark for the prize of the high calling of God in Christ Jesus" (Phil. 3:13).

I am sure Paul regretted how he persecuted the church. He must have regretted being part of the group that stoned Stephen, the first martyr for Jesus. Yet Paul chose to lay down those things he could not change. Stephen was with the Lord. Stephen understands now as Jesus understands. He would not have wanted Paul to live in regret. It is the same with our loved ones who have gone on to be with the Lord. They, too, understand and forgive all of our faults.

The heavenly perspective is similar to a mountaintop experience. We can see everything very clearly. We can see gaps in our defense against the enemy. We see the reason why people react the way they do.

Most of all, we must love now as Jesus loves. Regret can never change the situation. If Paul had lived in regret, it would have deprived the world and the church of all the good he went on to accomplish. This is a clear picture of Romans 8:28, where the Bible tells us "that all things work together for good to them that love God, to them who are the called according to his purpose."

Regret does not help those who have gone on to be with the Lord. It only hurts you and those who love you. God has a plan for your life. That might be hard to understand when you are filled with regret, but God is true to His Word.

He said, "For I know the thoughts that I think toward you, saith the Lord, thoughts of peace, and not of evil, to give you an expected end" (Jer. 29:11).

God has good plans for your life. Don't let regrets keep you from fulfilling them. Allow God to turn your failures into strengths. Paul needed God's grace to overcome his failures. Through this, Paul taught multitudes upon multitudes about the grace of God. *"All things work together for good."*

Benny told me, "God has a work for you to do, if you will focus on Jesus and finish strong."

THE STRONGHOLD OF GUILT

Another stronghold is guilt. Guilt will cause people to lash out at others. Often when a person is feeling guilty, whether he has cause to or not, he says things to make others around him angry. Whether consciously or subconsciously, he is so angry with himself that he would feel better if others were angry with him. He wants to punish himself, so he will do and say things that he really doesn't mean because of the guilt he carries. It takes a lot of understanding on the part of others to help the person through these times.

Marilyn's mother struggled horribly with guilt after the death of Ben and Lacey. She felt as if there were so many things left unsaid and undone. At first we did not know of her struggle, but Marilyn noticed her becoming more and more angry about things that made no sense at all. She was angry at everything and everyone. Finally, Marilyn decided to have a talk with her. What Marilyn discovered was the fact that her mother was carrying such guilt.

She told Marilyn, "When I am alone, all I do is cry. I can't seem to stop. There are so many things I wish I had done differently."

Marilyn shared with her about how we all feel like we could have done more. Then she shared how the kids were enjoying the splendors of heaven and that the guilt she carried was not affecting them.

"They loved you, and you loved them. All this guilt is only hurting you and your relationships with the rest of us."

They talked a long time that day, and a lot of healing took place. Don't allow guilt to take over your life. Leave the mistakes of your past in the past. Allow the Lord to relieve the burden of guilt and give you rest.

Jesus said, "Come unto me, all ye that labor and are heavy laden, and I will give you rest. Take my yoke upon you, and learn of me; for I am meek and lowly in heart: and ye shall find rest unto your souls. For my yoke is easy, and my burden is light" (Matt. 11:28–30).

"And I will restore to you the years that the locust hath eaten, the cankerworm, and the caterpillar, and the palmerworm...And ye shall eat in plenty, and be satisfied, and praise the name of the Lord your God."

—JOEL 2:25–26

14

Years of Restoration

T HE LORD WORKED MIGHTILY ON OUR BEHALF IN the arena of finances directly after the accident. In 1996, about a year-and-a-half later, God established the foundation of our calling into the ministry.

For years Marilyn and I had felt that at some time the Lord would use us in the ministry. Although we had served in many different capacities in the church, we always knew deep in our spirits that God had something else for us.

During a revival meeting at our church, the Lord spoke to my spirit about our ministry. That particular evening, the service was coming to a close when Belinda, one of the lead singers on the praise and worship team, rushed in. Having been out of town, she hurried in hoping to catch the last few minutes of the meeting. Belinda normally sang the lead part on a song that the visiting evangelist especially liked. Having spotted her from the platform, the evangelist said,

"Belinda, I know you just got here and haven't had time to warm up, and I know that you may not have practiced it in a long time. Yet, I just feel like you should sing 'Waymaker.'"

WAYMAKER*
by Percy Bady

He's a rock in a weary land
Shelter in the time of storm
He's an anchor I can hold on to
A foundation, stable and strong
I have no reason to doubt Him
I know too much about Him
For He is able; He's a waymaker

He is comfort in my deepest sorrow
Hope when I'm in despair
He is peace through ev'ry trial
Strength for my burdens to bear
Now He's never failed me
That's why I've got to tell you
He is able; He's a waymaker

How do you know He's a waymaker?
What has He done for you?
Has He brought you out without a doubt?
Has He saved your soul; has He made you
    whole?
Has He brought you through when you didn't
    know what to do?
He's a waymaker; oh, yes, He is!
He can make a way!

It was the first time I had ever heard the song, but as she sang, the Lord ministered to my spirit.

"I am calling you to go and tell My people that I am the Waymaker. You are to call your ministry Waymaker Ministries, for I made a way for you where there was no other way."

That night Waymaker Ministries was birthed in my spirit. Several months later I was asked to give my testimony at the men's fellowship meeting at our church. A young man and his father came down to the altar that night. The young man was saved, and his relationship with his father was strengthened. It was then that I knew the impact of pointing people to the Waymaker.

Then, on December 31, 1996, I gave my testimony to a small congregation of eight people in the Ocala National Forest. They had a little old church, but no pastor. I told Marilyn that the Lord was going to open doors of opportunity for us to minister.

She said, "That's fine for you; you might be called to preach, but not me. I think I should get a job. You preach, and I will work until the ministry can support us."

Things were getting rather tight financially, but I kept reminding Marilyn that all of our married life we had worked side by side. I didn't see where the Lord would have us work in the ministry any differ- ently. However, there was a house payment due of seven hundred dollars in just days. The weekend before we had to make that payment, I was asked to speak to a small congregation in a neighboring town. They were only meeting once a week, so they just needed me to speak that Sunday morning. Later that week, I also received a call from the overseer of that little church of eight in the forest. He wanted to know if we could come and share with the church again that Sunday evening. I told him we had an engagement for that morning but nothing for the evening and we would love to come. So Rachel, Marilyn and I went off that Sunday morning. It was one day before our house payment was due.

I gave my testimony that morning to the congregation. After I spoke, the assistant pastor took us out to lunch because the pastor was out of town. He told us during our meal, "We had decided we should pay you $75 for sharing with us this morning, but I really feel like that is not enough, so I have made the check out for $150."

We thanked him very much, and after finishing lunch we went home. Now the overseer from the Church in the Forest, (as it was called,) had already informed me that all they could afford to give us was fifty dollars. As Marilyn and I looked at that $150, she said, "This is a long way from $700, but, praise the Lord, He has never let us down yet."

Since I had already shared my testimony with the Church in the Forest, I encouraged Marilyn to share something with them. They were a very nice group of people, and there were only eight of them, which I was sure she could handle. Now Marilyn has always loved to teach, so she prepared a message titled, "The Mountains Around About Jerusalem," into which she weaved her side of the testimony.

She shared with them that night and was very well received. After the service was over, the gentleman in charge of the finances came up to me and said, "Here is the fifty dollars we promised you, plus someone wrote a check out to Waymaker Ministries for seventy dollars, so here is that also." While I was talking with this man, a woman came up to Marilyn and said she really felt led to give her something. It was in an offering envelope. Marilyn thanked her and stuck it in her Bible.

We walked out to the car and started home. Marilyn was driving that night, and we were talking about what to do about the house payment. The offerings we received that morning and that night totalled $270. We were just under $500 away from the amount needed for the mortgage payment.

Just about that time, Marilyn said, "Oh, look in my Bible. There is an envelope in it that a woman handed me before we left."

I opened it, and much to my surprise it was a check for $500.

I said, "Marilyn, it's $500."

She immediately started braking.

"Oh!" she exclaimed. "I accidentally dropped it when we were at the church, and I must have picked up the wrong envelope. I saw one on the floor where I was standing and picked it up. That one can't be for us. Is there another one in my Bible?"

I said, "No, Marilyn, there isn't. Besides, the check is made out to Waymaker Ministries."

Again, Jesus was showing us that He is our Waymaker in all things. The Lord showed us from the beginning of our ministry that He would meet our every need. He met the house payment and even left 10 percent for us to give back as a seed for Him to bless.

The man who was the overseer of the Church in the Forest again asked Marilyn and I if we would come back and speak with them. We spoke at the church numerous times over the next several months. The Lord gave us an opportunity to sharpen our skills among a people who accepted us as rookies in the ministry. During our short time with them we saw that little congregation grow from eight people to sometimes as many as thirty-five. However, the Lord had other things for us to do. Just as doors at this church opened for us, He sent them a retired pastor to be their shepherd, and our speaking services were no longer needed on a regular basis.

A friend of ours who used to write for the *Daytona Beach News Journal* and had followed our story from the first night. He helped us make fliers with a short version of our testimony. Somehow one of these fliers ended up on the desk of the editor of *Evangel Magazine*. This magazine is sent to all the Church of God churches (of Cleveland, Tennessee) around the world. They called our church and asked if they were familiar with us and our story. The secretary told them that she knew us well and gave them our home telephone number. That same day they called us to ask permission to run our story in their magazine. Of course, we agreed. When the article was printed, we received numerous invitations to speak in other churches.

God was doing more. As opportunities opened up, word got out in our town that we were traveling around giving our testimony. Again, God transcended denominational walls as we began to receive invitations from many of the churches that had helped us during our time of need. We spoke at Baptist churches, Wesleyan churches, Presbyterian churches, Assemblies of God churches, as well as some non-denominational churches.

The Lord raised us in the ministry little by little. As we continued to study His Word and seek Him, He increased our circle of ministry. We began to reach out and minister across the state. Then invitations

Years of Restoration

began to spread across the Southeast. Getting broader and broader, we finally stretched out across the United States.

As we traveled and spoke, we also had to increase our trust that the Lord would continue to provide every need. The car we were given after the accident was racking up the miles. It was no longer dependable for long trips.

In our home, we have a room that overlooks our driveway, where I often sit and pray. One day Marilyn came in the room as I was thanking the Lord for the new car He was going to give us.

I prayed, "Lord, I thank You for that beautiful, four-door sedan (I like to get specific) that is sitting in our driveway. You know, Lord, we need it to travel to the speaking engagements You have given us. I sure do thank You, Lord."

Marilyn began to laugh. "You had better start thanking Him for the money to make payments on a new car. You know a car just isn't going to appear in the driveway."

"Now, Marilyn," I began, "the Lord knows we need a car. I certainly do not want to be strapped down to a payment when we are trying to get this ministry launched. The Lord will provide the car. I told Him I would go, but He would have to make the way."

Day after day, I would look out over that driveway and thank the Lord for the new car that would one day be there. One day I received a call from Chris, a good friend of mine.

"Tom," Chris began, "the funniest thing just happened to me and my wife. I was out mowing the lawn when the Lord spoke to my heart. He told me he wanted me to buy you a car. So I stopped mowing and went into the house to speak to Diane. I said, 'Diane, the strangest thing just happened to me. I was mowing the lawn when the Lord spoke to me.'"

"Wait!" Diane yelled. "Don't tell me. I bet He told you to buy the Roses a car."

"How in the world did you know that?" he exclaimed.

"Because I was just mopping the floor, and He spoke the same thing to me."

Now, as Chris was telling me the story, I was very excited but a little apprehensive. Marilyn and I had many friends who could afford to buy us a car and never blink an eye, but Chris and Diane were not one of these. Chris had a good job and provided well for his family, but they did not have that kind of money.

I told Chris that was wonderful, but I added, "I really want you and Diane to spend some time praying about this before you try to do it."

The two of them sought the Lord for several weeks, yet they kept saying the Lord was asking them to step out in faith and do this. They did not have the money to buy a car outright, but they did have excellent credit and thought they wouldn't have any trouble financing one. It is one thing to give out of your abundance, but you had better hear from the Lord before you commit to payments. So all four of us—Chris, Diane, Marilyn and I—spent the next few weeks praying for God's will on the matter.

One afternoon we all decided to take the plunge. We went to a local car dealership where our friends had done business for years. The Lord opened the door by giving us a salesman who was involved in prison ministry part-time on the weekends. As we looked at cars, we all praised the Lord and had a great time of fellowship together. Chris told the salesman what he thought he could handle for payments. Low and behold, there was a beautiful, clean, four-door Grand Marquis on the lot. It had a large trunk for those longer trips. I also knew it would have a smooth ride, so we would not arrive at meetings all worn out. Chris and the salesman went in the back, worked on the numbers, and the deal was done several days later (it took that long because we put the car in the ministry's name).

Now, as I said, Chris had a good job, but there wasn't a whole lot of extra money. As it happened, after the deal was closed, it seemed like one thing after another started breaking down on them. First, it was their refrigerator. Then the central air went on the blink, which is a disaster in Florida. One thing after another kept going wrong. Even Diane's car broke down. Marilyn and I did not know what to do. Here, someone went out on a limb in faith for us. They were supposed to be blessed. I can't tell you how bad we felt. Yet they kept praising the Lord.

Diane reassured me one day, "I don't care if we have to live on peanut butter and jelly sandwiches. I still believe we did what the Lord asked us to do. We did not make this commitment to you and Marilyn. We made it to the Lord, and we will see it through."

During this time, Chris received a call from a competitor of the company for which he worked. They had heard of his integrity in the sales field and knew he had a good reputation with his customers. They wanted to know if he would come to work for them. Although Chris was not altogether happy where he worked—many of his co-workers used foul language, and the atmosphere in the office left much to be desired—he was still not a man to make a hasty decision. So he declined their offer. Things at home seemed to be getting harder and harder for them, and things he normally could shake off at work seemed harder also.

Finally, one evening the same competitor called, "Chris, our company is growing. We would again like to have you come on board with us. Just what would it take to persuade you to switch to our company?"

Chris now felt it was time to make the move. The new company's offer allowed Chris to make the car payment out of the increase of a single week of his pay. To top it off, he discovered that the owners and management were Christians who prayed before they started their meetings.

Chris and Diane never missed a payment. Chris is the top salesman at work; with his Christmas bonus this year, he was able to pay the car off one year early. They were determined to stay focused on Jesus, no matter how their circumstances looked. Then Jesus made a way for them and blessed them more then they could have imagined.

As we began to mature in the ministry, we would speak for several days at a time in the same location. It was really refreshing for us to be able to share beyond our testimony. In July 1999, *Charisma* magazine, a magazine that reaches hundreds of thousands of readers, ran our story. From that point on, the ministry branched off in several different directions. We not only received numerous requests from other magazines to run the story that *Charisma* published (all of which *Charisma* graciously allowed), but we also began receiving invitations to speak on a number of different radio broadcasts. From small local stations, to KKLA, which is the largest Christian talk radio station in the United States. KKLA radio programs are aired simultaneously on 102 affiliate stations through four satellite hook-ups and over the world wide web. They gave us a forty-five-minute interview along with live call-in questions. This was probably the hardest thing we had ever done in ministry. Trying to answer the questions of hurting people on the spot was so difficult. The only thing we could do was to try to point them to Jesus, the Waymaker.

Shortly after that, a producer from the "Decision Today" program, part of the Billy Graham Association, conducted a phone interview with us. They took segments of that interview and interjected portions of it into several different programs, using bits and pieces as needed. If they happened to be talking about forgiveness, then they used that part of the interview, or if it were on God's love in the middle of difficult situations, then they would insert that portion of the interview.

Not long after our testimony appeared in *Charisma*, we received a request to come to Nigeria. When Marilyn and I read the request, we felt the Spirit of the Lord and were quite touched with the pastor's heart-felt plea. During the past year we had received requests from all over the world (including Africa), but this one seemed different. We decided we would seriously consider going and committed the matter to prayer.

As we prayed about going to Nigeria, we decided to research some facts on about the country. The country of Nigeria is a little larger than the state of Texas with a population of 120 million people, which makes it the most populated country in Africa. Travel in Nigeria is not only expensive, but it can also be very dangerous. The cities are extremely large and dirty. It also has one of the highest death rates of children in the world. Twenty percent of their children die before the age of five. When we saw this statistic we knew why the Lord had moved upon our hearts to go.

Although we wanted to respond favorably to the pastor's request to come to Warri, Nigeria, we were concerned about how to get from Lagos (the city where we would arrive by plane), to Warri, which is about three hundred miles away. Again, the reports were bad. The state department issued a bulletin stating the dangers of traveling in all of Nigeria, especially Lagos, (which is the only city that receives international flights,) and said it was not worth the danger to see "the ugliest city in the world." Most taxis were unreliable, as well as dangerous. There had been reports of people getting into taxis and never reaching their final destinations. Also, it was extremely hard to rent reliable vehicles.

I wrote the pastor of Warri with a number of questions, but the hand of the Lord moved even before we had time to receive a reply. One week after receiving the invitation, we had meetings scheduled in Maderian, Mississippi. Due to Hurricane Floyd, which was passing by Florida and causing evacuations, we decided to leave a day early and visit with friends in Carthage, Mississippi. From there we called the pastor of a church where we had spoken several times.

While talking with this pastor I mentioned we were considering going to Nigeria. The pastor told us a church member had a man from Nigeria staying with her, and the pastor set up a lunch date for us to meet him. Wouldn't you know that this man pastored one of the largest churches—2,500 adults—in Lagos, a city of 12 million people.

He not only extended an invitation for us to come and minister at his church, but also to the body of Christ in Nigeria at large. He told us that some of the members of his church would meet us at the airport with singing. They would bring us to his home where we would rest for a couple of days to recover from jet lag. Then he would arrange for us to speak to many of the pastors of Lagos. Then, after we spoke in Lagos, he would personally have someone drive us to Warri to be received by the pastor there. He also assured us that upon our return he would receive us back into his home and see that we got safely on the plane for our return trip. He said he would contact the pastor in Warri and make all the arrangements. Before we had a chance to even respond he had answered every question I had asked in my letter to the pastor in Warri.

We discovered that when the Lord is in something, He covers all the bases. Finally, in February 2000, we took our first overseas ministry trip to Nigeria, West Africa, and what an experience! I would like to tell you it was an exotic destination, but it wasn't.

We ministered fifteen times in fourteen days. Although the living conditions were the worst I have ever seen, even worse than war-torn Vietnam, we fell in love with the people.

Rachel accompanied us, and she was astounding. During our stay in Nigeria, we often had no running water in which to bathe, and when there was water, it was a cold trickle. The majority of our stay was in Lagos, where the sewer systems for twelve million people have not been functional for over two years. The sewage ran in open gutters in the streets, and there had not been any type of garbage collections for years. Therefore, there were mountains of garbage burning all over the city. The stench was unbelievable. Yet Rachel, now thirteen years old and quite particular about her surroundings, never muttered a complaint. In fact, she would often awake at night and pray for the upcoming meetings.

The prayer lines were tremendous in all of our services. We prayed for just about every disease imaginable. Often the children wanted us to pray for wisdom, or simply for a blessing over them. So, we asked Rachel if she would pray for some of these needs, which she did with great joy. We found her holding children and pouring out such compassion for them. She truly was an asset to us. Previously, while ministering in the States, she always seemed to hold back, never wanting to join us on the platform. But now, under such difficult circumstances, she flourished.

When we left Africa, she told us she had such mixed feelings and was not sure if she would ever want to return. But a few weeks later, her youth leader asked her to share some of the experiences she had in Africa. She was so nervous, Marilyn and I were beginning to wonder if she would be able to do it. But fortunately, she had many pictures to show—she loves to photograph the meetings, so this has always been her job in the ministry. Once she got up in front of the group and began to show the photos, everything seemed to flow. You could see her beginning to relax and enjoy herself. Sharing those memories must have impacted her because several days later she told Marilyn, "Mom, I thought when we left Nigeria I would never want to return. Everything was so hard. Yet I think about the people all the time. I know if you ever return I will want to go with you."

God truly has done a work in Rachel's life. Many of our friends have mentioned the change they have witnessed in her. After the accident she became so withdrawn. But because of what the Lord has accomplished in her, today she is full of enthusiasm for everything. She loves school, attending almost every function held on school grounds. She sings in the youth choir at church and is part of the drama team. And yet, she still seems to find time to join in activities held by several other churches.

On our return trip from Africa, we were able to minister in Europe for a little over two weeks. We spoke to a new group of Christians who had fled to Germany from Iraq for political asylum. They spoke Persian but had a fantastic interpreter. We also ministered to a couple from Afghanistan who had lost a child to small-arms fire in the war with Russia. We spoke to a German congregation and a number of U.S. Army Service Men's Centers. The Lord just opened door after door. We could have stayed longer. We had more invitations to speak, but we had already made arrangements for our return home.

Before leaving Europe, there was one more thing that we felt we needed to do. When Rachel had learned that we would be in Europe, she had asked repeatedly if we could go to Paris—the dream of many a thirteen-year-old girl. We were not sure if we would be able to accomplish this. But when we witnessed the way she handled herself in Africa, never complaining, we knew then that we would do all we could to see that she made it to Paris. And we did it! The Paris trip was only for three days, including travel time, but we had a wonderful time.

Upon our return to the States, we were blessed with the opportunity to do an interview with the *700*

Club. Two days after our return, they had a crew come to our home, and we did a day of taping for an upcoming story on our testimony. It was difficult, but we thanked the Lord for yet another opportunity to share with others the way that *Jesus will make a way where there is no other way!*

Remember my sister, Vickie, who was driving the car the night of the accident? After enduring five years of her own trials, she was gloriously and wondrously saved. As of January 2000, I was able to personally lead her to the Lord. She truly is a new creation in Christ Jesus. As for the other two girls who were injured in the accident, they both survived. However, we have very little contact with either of them. We do pray for them on a regular basis and ask the Lord to keep His hand on their lives.

"Rejoice with them that do rejoice, and weep with them that weep."

—ROMANS 12:15

15

Words to a Friend

OT LONG AGO I WAS TALKING WITH A PASTOR'S wife who lost a son to AIDS. She was saying how so many people brought food, "but what I needed more than food was someone to sit down and talk to me while I ate the food, but no one knew what to say. Really, they did not need to say anything. I just desperately wanted someone to talk to."

When tragedy strikes, all the promises of God hurt. All the good clichés—"Well, you know they are in a better place"—hurt. The one thing hurting people need the most is your friendship. They need someone to talk to.

You don't need to know what to say. In fact, the less you say the better. Let them do the talking. Often they will want to talk about their loved ones. If their loved ones did well in sports, they might want to talk about that. If they were good singers, they will want to talk about that. Your job, if you want to minister to them, will be to just listen.

Don't try to cut them off from talking about things

that might make both of you cry. Sometimes that is just what is needed—a good cry. At other times, they might want to laugh and talk about other things. This also is OK. Don't always feel like you have to drag things up. If they are feeling good that day, then thank God for it. There will be another day of crying just around the corner.

The person who helped Marilyn the most when we lost our children was only a casual acquaintance. Having lost a father amidst difficult circumstances, she knew how much Marilyn needed a friend. She became that friend.

Marilyn used to tell me, "I feel as if I could share anything with her and she would not judge my feelings."

She would just let her get it out. Some days they would laugh together. Other days, they would cry. She became one of Marilyn's closest friends. You do not have to be a close friend in the beginning to be the person the Lord uses to help someone else carry their cross. God never intended for us to carry the cross of tragedy alone. David had Jonathan, Paul had Silas, and even Jesus had Simon, who came along-side of him and helped him shoulder the weight of the cross.

Lend your shoulder to someone in need today. God will bless you for it.

"O death, where is thy sting? O grave, where is thy victory? ...Thanks be to God, which giveth us the victory through our Lord Jesus Christ."

— 1 Corinthians 15:55, 57

16

Two Graves on a Hill

D O YOU REMEMBER THOSE TWO GRAVES I TOLD you Marilyn and I purchased that first Christmas after we lost the children? Well, right before going to Africa I told Marilyn I wanted to go out to the cemetery. When we got out there, we visited the kids' graves. Then I walked up the hill to the two plots I had purchased for us.

As I stood on top of the grave that all the doctors felt sure I would be occupying by now, I thanked the Lord one more time for what He did that day for me at the DeLand Sanctuary Church of God. I thanked Him for healing my body, but most of all I praised Him for what He did for me that day at Calvary. Then I began to do a little dance, right there on those graves.

You see, I can dance on my grave today because one day in a church in the small town of DeLand, Florida, Jesus of Nazareth, passed my way. He made a way where there seemed to be no other way.

Most of the time everyone wants to hear about the miracle heart I received, how I was expected to die and Jesus showed up and touched me. Yet, in retrospect, I recognize that I had been sick for quite some time. At one time my heart worked at half of its capacity, and I was a happy man. After the first heart failure, my heart was at 30 percent, but I could still say I was a happy man. It was when I lost my children my heart was broken.

To me the greatest miracle was not the healing of my physical heart. It was when Jesus mended our broken hearts. Besides our salvation, this is the greatest miracle of all. I know I will never see my son graduate from the Air Force Academy, which was his dream. I will never see Lacey become a large animal veterinarian and train horses, which was her dream.

There is, however, one thing I have seen—our children in the arms of a loving Savior. I still miss them—and I will until that day we are together again—yet Jesus has given me beauty for ashes, the oil of joy for mourning, the garment of praise for the spirit of heaviness; that I might be called a tree of righteousness, the planting of the Lord, that He might be glorified.

As Marilyn and I have walked through the valley of decision, the Lord has been true to His word—He has indeed become our hope and our strength. And He will do the same for you!

Are you in the valley of decision? If you are, the decisions you make can, and will, affect eternity. Perhaps the circumstances in your life seem unbearable. Perhaps you have grown cold in your relationship with the Lord or have become angry with Him. If so, let me encourage you to return to the Lord, for He loves you. It doesn't matter what you have said or how you have felt; He still loves you. It is no coincidence that you are reading this book. The Lord is calling you back into relationship with Him.

Many of you are struggling with unforgiveness and have carried it with you for too long. Please remember that forgiveness is not a feeling; it is a choice. When you choose to forgive, God brings the feelings. Trust Him today and forgive. The Lord will be faithful to help you.

Others of you have never received the free gift of salvation through Jesus Christ. If you have never given your life to the Lord Jesus, call on Him today. For "whosoever shall call on the name of he Lord shall be saved" (Acts 2:21). Jesus will not only save you from sin, He will also walk with you through the valley of decision.

Stay close to the Lord and press on. He loves you! He will make a way where there is no way. For He truly is the Waymaker.

▶ Ben Rose,
9 years old

◀ Lacey Rose,
12 years old

▲ Tom
preaching the
Gospel in a
church in
Lagos,
Nigeria

▶ Tom,
Rachel and
Marilyn
sharing their
testimony in
West Africa

▲ Rachel ministering to
African children

▶ Rachel Rose, 14 years old

▲ The Rose family in 2000—Rachel, Marilyn and Tom

For more information or to schedule the Roses
for speaking engagements, contact:

WAYMAKER MINISTRIES
P.O. Box 473
DeLand, FL 32721-0473

Email: wrose3@cfl.rr.com

Visit our website at:
www.Waymakerministries.org

Other books by Thomas and Marilyn Rose:
The Mountains Around Jerusalem
The Keeper of the Bride

Also available:
Teaching and testimony cassettes